Praise for *M*

"I love how Anne Wilson invites us into the cracks and crevices of her life and how she built her life on Jesus. The story behind 'My Jesus' is much more than a few months process of writing a song. *My Jesus* is personal, and it takes you on a journey through some of the most foundational parts of Anne's life that develop into a large picture where it is so clear that God was the artist of it all. As I read through each page, I felt like I was at coffee with Anne, hearing her story."

—Sadie Robertson Huff, author, speaker, and founder of Live Original

"The song 'My Jesus' has impacted so many of our lives in such important ways. Reading this book, being in the moments with Anne and her family, and hearing her faith rise up when her heart was broken, Anne has told a true and deep story that we all need to read."

—Annie F. Downs, *New York Times* bestselling author of *That Sounds Fun*

"Getting to know Anne Wilson and her family over the last couple of years and seeing her journey as a young artist has been so special. We've celebrated many milestones and victories with her as God continues to use her music in really powerful ways in the lives of so many. It's inspiring to me to know that these triumphs were born out of great personal tragedy and loss. Jesus truly is the Great Redeemer! I pray you'll be as impacted as I have been by Anne's incredible story."

—Mike Weaver of Big Daddy Weave

"It has been an honor to get to know Anne during our time on the road together. Each night I saw how her story touched so many lives, and I know this book is going to impact so many more for the glory of God. Anne's story of personal loss, restored through God's provision, is a must read."

—Zach Williams, two-time Grammy Award winner

"Anne has been blessed and burdened with the weight of incredible testimony, the kind that helps us believe in the redeeming power of Jesus. The pages before you are evidence of one who knows Christ and one whose desire is to use everything she has to make Him known. This story is special, and I know those who read it will be encouraged by the depth of God's grace shown to Anne and her family."

—Jordan St. Cyr, songwriter and recording artist of the Billboard #1 single "Weary Traveler"

"Wow! I am convinced that as you journey with Anne through the pages of this book, her authentic passion and purity of heart will open your eyes to see Jesus in a more tangible and accessible way than ever before. If He is not already, I believe her Jesus will become your Jesus."

—M. Cameron McDonald, pastor of Remnant House Church

FROM HEARTACHE TO HOPE

ANNE WILSON

With Marcie Maggart

An Imprint of Thomas Nelson

My Jesus

Published in Nashville, Tennessee, by Nelson Books, an imprint of Thomas Nelson. Nelson Books and Thomas Nelson are registered trademarks of HarperCollins Christian Publishing, Inc.

Published in association with the literary agency of WTA Media, LLC., Franklin, Tennessee.

Thomas Nelson titles may be purchased in bulk for educational, business, fundraising, or sales promotional use. For information, please email SpecialMarkets@ThomasNelson.com.

Library of Congress Cataloging-in-Publication Data

Names: Wilson, Anne, 2002- author.
Title: My Jesus : from heartache to hope / Anne Wilson with Marcie Maggart.
Description: Nashville : Thomas Nelson, 2022. | Summary: "In My Jesus, Anne Wilson shares her remarkable journey through the loss of her brother and the surprising moment she heard God's voice calling her to do the unexpected--sing and create music that would draw people to Him, which then birthed her #1 hit song, "My Jesus.""-- Provided by publisher.
Identifiers: LCCN 2022019449 (print) | LCCN 2022019450 (ebook) | ISBN 9781400238224 (trade paperback) | ISBN 9781400238231 (ebook)
Subjects: LCSH: Consolation. | Bereavement—Religious aspects--Christianity. | Grief--Religious aspects--Christianity. | Contemporary Christian music--History and criticism.
Classification: LCC BV4909 .W56 2022 (print) | LCC BV4909 (ebook) | DDC 248.8/6--dc23/eng/20220720
LC record available at https://lccn.loc.gov/2022019449
LC ebook record available at https://lccn.loc.gov/2022019450

Printed in the United States of America

22 23 24 25 26 LSC 10 9 8 7 6 5 4 3 2 1

To my precious brother in heaven, Jacob

Contents

Foreword

I REMEMBER RECEIVING THE PHONE CALL. IT WAS A familiar request for my line of work as a songwriter in Nashville. "There's a new artist and she's really talented," the record label said. "Would you be willing to write a song with her?"

Although most people might know me as a recording artist, my earliest days in Nashville were mostly spent behind the scenes as a writer. And while these days I get to make records and tour around the world singing my own songs, I've always felt called to champion other young artists as they share their story with the world—one three-minute song at a time. So I accepted the invitation to write with a new artist named Anne Wilson.

Our appointment began the way most do, with coffee and conversation. I learned about Anne's love of Jesus, Dunkin' Donuts iced coffee, country music, and the great state of Kentucky. Now, at its worst, a songwriting session can feel like a stress-filled, pressure-packed environment that leaves you insecure and convinced you've chosen the wrong profession. It's difficult to be vulnerable and honest in front of people you're close to, let alone a stranger you met only an hour ago! But that's what songwriting takes: vulnerability and honesty. And those things are only accessible to us in safe places. At its best, the songwriting room can transform into that safe place where you're free to wear your heart on your sleeve. On this day a safe place was found.

I was deeply moved as eighteen-year-old Anne shared the same powerful story you are about to read in this book. A story of faith, family, tragedy, and redemption. The next thing I knew, we were singing, crying, and writing a song called "My Jesus." I smile as I think about how that song has gone on to move the hearts of so many people around the world. Like the song, this book is a word-by-word reminder that there is one who can change your life. One name above all names. And in that one name we find the answer to all of life's most difficult questions:

> Where can I find a firm foundation when the world around me is crumbling? *Jesus.*
> Where can I find comfort in the middle of my mourning? *Jesus.*
> Who offers me rest when I'm past the point of weary? *Jesus.*
> Who can make a broken heart beat again? *Jesus.*
> Who loves me unconditionally? *Jesus*
> Who can work all things for my good? *Jesus.*

Just as Anne invited me into her story that day in the songwriting room, she is now inviting *you* into her story with this powerful book. And like any great story, this is one we can all see ourselves in. Every life will be touched by trials, pain, loss, even grief. I am praying this book provides the same safe place for you that we discovered that day in the studio. Invite Jesus to meet you in that safe place and rest assured, He will. He stands at the door of your heart and knocks. Let Him in and let my Jesus change your life.

—Matthew West, award-winning singer-songwriter, author, and cofounder of popwe

ONE

Faith Like a Child

I SAT ON THE FRONT STEP WITH MY BACKPACK LOADED for adventure, tapping my tennis shoe on the concrete. My older brother, Jacob, was supposed to pick me up at 3:00 that autumn afternoon, but he was late as usual. I had hurried through my eighth-grade homework so we could leave as early as possible. I was not surprised Jacob was late, but I was a bit annoyed.

I wanted every minute with him I could get. And whatever last-moment idea had caught his attention was stealing precious minutes from our time together. Finally, Jacob's gray Ford pickup turned the corner onto our street. I jumped up with a grin.

"Hey, Annie," he called through his rolled-down window. "Ready to go?"

"I was ready thirty minutes ago!" I pretended to still be annoyed, but I wasn't. Jacob's presence always lifted my mood. I hopped into the passenger seat and buckled up, eager to be on the road.

"Can I turn on the radio?" I asked, reaching for the knob.

"Only if you turn on country music." He gave me a playful wink as he backed out of the driveway. We were on our way. The hour-long drive to the Wilson Family Farm was always filled with country music and laughter when I was with Jacob. My brother made me laugh more than anyone else, and I felt carefree sitting by his side as we drove through the curvy backroads of Kentucky.

Wilson Family Farm belongs to Daddy's side of the family and is my favorite place on earth. I love the variety of the land—the open fields, the heavily wooded hills, the cool valleys, and the picturesque trails winding through it all. Granddaddy lives out on the farm with his wife, Jan, and oversees every inch. We have chickens, pigs, donkeys, cows, and horses. The property is also home to several barns, a hayloft, and the farmhouse. With more than five hundred acres to explore, Wilson Farm offers both fun and solitude. I had been going out there for as long as I could remember. Though we lived in the suburbs, I had the heart of a country girl and often wished I could live on the farm.

When we arrived that day, Jacob and I headed straight to the barn where we saddled up two horses. We often hiked the trails on the farm, but that day we would explore them by horseback. Riding horses always felt more adventurous to me—like we could do anything we set our minds to. And that day we decided to ride up High Point Mountain, the name our family gave to one of my favorite spots on the farm. From the top you can look down over the entire property and out across the horizon for miles.

Jacob led the way as we rode up the winding trail. Every few seconds he looked back to check on me. I pretended his watchfulness irritated me, but it actually made me feel safe. I knew my brother would protect me no matter what happened. Once we reached the summit, we tied our horses to a tree and sat down on a patch of soft grass to relax.

Those moments on the mountain were always the best part of the whole excursion for me. Jacob and I were the only two people around for miles. Staring out over the blue-tinted grass covering the open Kentucky fields below, we shared our dreams for the future. I felt grateful that Jacob let me into his world. Even with eight years between us, he made me feel like we were best friends.

"Well, Annie," Jacob said after a few minutes of comfortable silence, "how are your plans for space travel coming along?"

"Very funny," I said, rolling my eyes. "You'll see. Someday I'll be an astronaut and wave at you from space." Jacob laughed, but in a way that told me he was proud of me for working toward my dream. I was following the advice he always gave to my sister, Elizabeth, and me: dream big, work hard, and be kind.

"All right," he said. "Tell me about it again. What makes you want to go to space?"

"I don't even know where to begin," I said. Soon I found the words to explain how the wonders of the heavens God created intrigued me. I lay back on the grass and stared up at the light-blue sky. The breeze was swift, and the clouds moved quickly. "Don't you just want to see what all God has made out there in the sky?"

Jacob didn't reply. Instead, he lay back and joined me in staring up at the heavens. I listened to the wind moving the gold and orange leaves of the trees below us and thought how perfect this moment was. Then I turned to Jacob and asked him about college—what classes he was taking and what books he was reading. His life, like the sky, fascinated me. In many ways, I hoped to be just like him one day. He told me he had just added a political science major to his current literature major.

"What is political science for?" I asked, wrinkling my nose.

"So I can become a lawyer, Annie," he said, lacing his fingers behind his neck. "I want to find a way to help people through my profession—and that one feels right."

"Well, I think you'll be an amazing lawyer," I said without hesitation. "You are so smart and so good with words. It's perfect for you."

I was proud of my big brother. Entwined with Jacob's adventurous spirit was an old soul. God had given him extra doses of bravery and energy, but also wisdom and a love of learning. He enjoyed studying noble leaders, like Winston Churchill. Churchill, the British prime minister during World War II, stood up to evil and was a man of great wisdom and leadership. Jacob devoured the writings of C. S. Lewis and J.R.R. Tolkien, getting lost in their worlds of fantasy as well as their ideas on the Christian life. My brother was a deep thinker, an insatiable reader, and a beautiful writer—a creative soul who thrived in the great outdoors.

Shoot for the Stars

The following summer, my mother and I walked out of the large glass doors of the Kennedy Space Center Visitor Complex in Cape

Canaveral. We turned to look at each other. "You know this is what I'm going to do," I said.

"I know," she said, tears in her eyes. "And I have to be okay with it." My mom knew me better than anyone else, so she recognized the passion in my heart. My parents, Kent and Lynn Wilson, encouraged all three of their children to pursue their dreams. Jacob, eight years my senior, was in college. My sister, Elizabeth, whom we call Liz, was eighteen and already following her dreams of clothing design, selling apparel through her thriving Etsy shop. But I was the youngest, and letting go was hard. Mom had raised me to believe anything was possible, and she knew my determination. Once I put my mind to something, I did it. I wanted to go to space.

Even as a toddler, I would stare up at the heavens in wonder. Everything in the sky fascinated me. But I was truly hooked in seventh grade when my science teacher, Mrs. Powell, taught us astronomy. From the hard plastic chairs of our school in Lexington, Kentucky, we explored God's massive universe—the planets and stars an expression of God's creativity. Mrs. Powell's excitement over God's intricate design was contagious, and I caught it. I became curious about many aspects of space and was intent on learning all I could about the heavens.

My parents not only encouraged my passion, they fanned it into flame. On that scorching summer day, my mom and dad went out of their way on our family vacation to allow me to see NASA firsthand. I was in my own world of delight exploring the history of space travel, listening to the tour guide describe exhilarating shuttle launches, and learning from a retired astronaut about the hard work and incredible joy of going to space. My nerve endings seemed to tingle as I imagined the rush of exiting our own atmosphere and viewing earth from the heavens.

My mom did not have the same thrilling experience I did, however. She was instead remembering the heartbreak of the space shuttle *Challenger* tragedy and reliving the day she watched the shuttle explode from her college student center. She had stood rooted to the ground, gasping in horror along with thousands of other Americans at the tragic sight. With these memories filling her mind, my mom realized that my ambitions involved great risk.

"I'm excited for you, Anne, even though I feel nervous about it," Mom explained. Our eyes, squinting under the relentless Florida sun, locked together for a brief moment. "You are only on loan to me from God, sweetheart," she said softly. "I've always known that. If His plans for you involve going to space, I'll trust Him with that, and I'll help you do it."

Leaving the NASA headquarters was a bittersweet moment. I was more resolved than ever that this was what I wanted for my life. And my mom and dad resolved to trust God and let me go for it. Most parents tell their kids to aim for the stars; in my case, I was taking that advice literally.

When school resumed in the fall, I took double classes as a freshman so I could be prepared academically. I worked incredibly hard and gave up extra time with friends to make good grades so I could get into a college in line with my dreams. I had my eyes set on universities in Florida, nearer to Cape Canaveral than my own landlocked state of Kentucky.

Raised with Wonder

With Jacob and Liz as my childhood best friends, I developed a love of imagination and adventure early in my life. I went along with almost any idea they came up with, and I loved every minute of it. But it also became apparent that, unlike them, I relish order. I love to plan and prepare. If you need a logistics manager, to-do lists, or detailed plans, I'm your girl. In contrast to my siblings' free-spirited ways, I was the rule follower and the little boss who tried to keep my siblings on track.

I used to plan exactly what time we needed to leave the house to be on time wherever we were going. And if we had a free weekend or a vacation, I mapped out every minute for the whole family.

"But Annie," Jacob once teased me, "what if we don't want to do what you have planned for us on vacation?"

"Well, Jacob," I retorted, tilting my head with all the sass I could muster, "it's already written down, so you have to." Once my plans were down on paper, they were as good as done in my mind.

"Well, little Annie," Jacob replied, raising his eyebrows, "you need to understand that we might want to have our own plan . . . or no plan."

"Well, you're not the boss of *me*!" In this family of free spirits, I was doing my best to bring some structure.

We had only one TV in our home, which was tucked away in my parents' bedroom, so we had to create our own entertainment and adventure in our giant unfinished basement. My parents gave us free rein to transform the basement into any fantasy world we could imagine. It was a magical place for us, and we spent countless hours playing down there.

One year, my dad and Jacob transformed the basement into a basketball court, where Jacob could practice his dribbling and lay-ups while releasing some of his ample energy. He drilled the basketball goal into the wall, and my dad helped him spray lines on the concrete floor. When the court was finished, Jacob spent hours down there playing, the constant yet comforting sounds of a dribbling basketball echoing through our home. Sometimes Daddy would join him on his homemade court, and they'd shoot hoops late into the night, especially throughout the winter.

Another year my parents helped Liz and me turn the basement into a cupcake shop furnished with a table, chairs, and an Easy Bake Oven for making tiny culinary masterpieces. Using her artistic talents, Liz hand-painted a banner for our shop, complete with little hearts all over it, and our name: Cutie Pie Cupcakes. The tempting scents of chocolate and cinnamon invited many a friend and neighbor to sample our delicious treats. (Today Liz runs her own clothing business, and I can't help but wonder if running Cutie Pie Cupcakes is what ignited her entrepreneurial spirit.)

My favorite basement renovation was the time we turned it into the home of the March girls from the book *Little Women.* Along with our friends Emma and Sarah, we dressed up as the March sisters and, with our best manners, attempted to act just like them. In the darkness of the basement, we'd light candles and let the wax drip down onto the floor while we played in the soft light for hours on end. By the flickering light we wrote letters and carefully sealed them with wax. The girls and I nibbled on little rolls from our local bakery as we sipped our tea. Then we retired to our bedrooms made from cardboard boxes and gazed out through the "windows" drawn with chalk on the cold concrete wall.

Being the youngest, I always wanted to be Amy. Liz was Jo, and Emma was Meg. My best friend, Sarah, was sometimes willing to be Beth, but other times she didn't want to play that character, for reasons I won't spoil if you haven't read the book. At those times she chose instead to be a red-eyed fox, a character concocted from her own imagination, that snuck in through the window to liven up our story with a bit of suspense!

The Great Outdoors

I believe God gives siblings a special connection they share with no one else on earth, to be each other's teachers, confidants, and friends. And this was very true of the Wilson siblings. We loved our times in the basement, but if Jacob had his way, all our adventures would have occurred outdoors. Our home has a spacious and well-kept backyard, ideal for games of make-believe. We especially loved playing in "the jumping tree" in our backyard. Climbing up that great willow tree required a team effort. Jacob would launch himself into the air and grab one of the many long limbs hanging from the tree.

"Here you go, girls!" he'd holler. "Jump on up!" As Jacob held down the branch, we would grab hold and pull ourselves up. Then the three of us would climb the tree together until we found our perfect spots. We spent hours in the branches of that tree, sharing secrets, stories, and jokes. Jacob could make me laugh until my sides hurt.

When the heavy spring rains caused the creek to swell, Jacob would lead Elizabeth and me down to the water to build miniature rafts out of cardboard, leaves, and branches. Once we were each satisfied with our boats, we would race them down the rushing current. That creek is also where Jacob taught us to catch crawdads.

He would kneel by the flowing water and do his best to bolster our confidence as we hunted the little freshwater crustaceans.

"Come on, Anne," he coaxed. "Grab that one! Grab him firmly on his body so his little claws can't reach you." I reached out for the crawdad but quickly retracted my hand as the creature scurried away in his backward fashion. He looked so aggressive with his sharp claws and quick flashing movements.

Jacob chuckled. "You don't have to be afraid of that little thing. He's afraid of *you*!" I took him at his word, gathered my courage, and tried again. *Success!* I giggled with joy as I proudly held my prize up for Jacob to see.

One winter Jacob conceived the brilliant idea of making an ice-skating rink in our backyard. When the temperature dipped below freezing, he removed all the furniture from the back patio. He gathered a bucket of hot water and a mop and proceeded to mop a layer of water onto the concrete. After the first layer was frozen, he mopped on another layer, and another, until a thick layer of ice had formed.

When the rink was finally ready, the three of us donned our warmest coats and hats. We shoved our feet into our skates and tied them tightly around our ankles. Liz and I ventured out onto the ice slowly, but Jacob went all in, sliding across the slick patio and pulling us with him. He put his hands on our waists and pushed us around the ice.

"Stop it!" we yelled, laughing. But he knew as well as we did that his stopping was the last thing we actually wanted. In fact, we begged him to do it for us the following year, and from then on Jacob made us an ice rink every year until he graduated.

Pictures of Jesus

That one little TV in our home, though rarely watched, did play an important role in my life. As a little girl, I would crawl onto the foot of my parents' bed and curl up to view *The Gospel of John*, a movie my family enjoyed watching together. I've seen the film enough times that I've nearly memorized it word for word. I felt the deep emotions portrayed in this telling of Jesus' time on earth and watched transfixed as Jesus used common, everyday things like dirt and spit to heal a blind man. I loved to see the Savior interact with people in the middle of their ordinary lives. It made Jesus seem so real to me, and I wished I could be one of those kids who sat on His lap and talked to Him face-to-face.

My mom tells me that I have always seemed to have a compassionate, empathetic spirit—I feel what others feel. So when the movie neared the scene where Jesus died on the cross, I refused to watch. I knew the pain and anguish that was coming, and I could not handle even the thought of it. So I would fast-forward right through to His resurrection. I refused to watch my sweet Jesus go through that agony, because I felt it so deeply in my little-girl heart. Even at that tender age, I loved Him. And as I came to Him with my childlike faith, I am sure He delighted in my love.

From this film, I first recognized the truth that Jesus knew suffering. He endured pain that I cannot imagine and never wanted to glimpse as a little girl. Jesus walked His own road of suffering, and therefore, I know He empathizes with mine.

When we were young, my mom used to tuck us all into our beds every night and pray over us. "Oh, I love you so good!" she would say, holding us close. "You are my breath, my oxygen, my everything." Then she would sit back, stroke our hair, and add, "As much as I love you, honey, God loves you so much more."

My siblings and I never doubted our mother's love. She loves extravagantly, holding little back. Experiencing my mom's very tangible love in those moments helped me to understand, as much as a little girl can, the great love of the Father.

My earthly father—my daddy—also showed me glimpses of God's love every day of my life. Daddy is the rock of our family. For me, he has always been a safety net—the person I could go to when I was in trouble or in need of assistance. If I got hurt, he comforted me. If I needed help on homework, he was the first one I went to. When I needed advice about anything, from drama with friends to how to understand the Bible, I knew I could talk to Daddy about it. He listened without judgment.

I'll always remember the morning of my fourth birthday. On

that special day, my daddy, my hero, came to carry me downstairs in grand style. "Happy birthday, sweetheart," he said, greeting me with a big hug and a kiss. Then he swung me up onto his strong shoulders. I was the birthday princess, seeing the world from that safe perch. Up there I could see what he saw, far above the smaller vantage point of my usual four-year-old height. To this day, I still run to Daddy for help to see a new perspective and feel the comfort of his love. In fact, I am convinced that without the foundation of love and faith both my parents laid for us, we could not have survived the storms that lay ahead—at least not with our hearts and belief intact.

Grounded in Truth

I grew up attending Tates Creek Presbyterian Church with my family from the time I was four years old. As I sat in the pews of this beautiful church, the knowledge of God and His Word began to solidify in my mind under the teachings of Reverend Mark Randle. I used to sit in my Sunday school classroom soaking in the stories about Jesus, excited to tell my mom all about them at Sunday dinner. As I listened to the sermons and sang the old sacred hymns, I learned who God is and what His Word says. Standing with my family, hymnal in hand, I would gaze up at the cross as all our voices blended together and proclaimed the truth in songs such as "Great Is Thy Faithfulness."

At that time in my life, hymns were the only kind of worship music I knew, and the declarations of God's faithfulness and majesty went deep into my soul. From there, the Holy Spirit can draw them up anytime He desires. Throughout my life, the Lord has often brought the words and melodies of these beloved hymns to my mind, even inspiring me as a songwriter.

By the time I was in junior high, I had a wealth of knowledge about Christianity, but all I'd learned was still mostly at a head level. I knew so much about the Lord, but I had yet to experience Him for myself at an intimate heart level. It was on the first day of seventh grade that I had an unexpected encounter with God. I was attending Veritas Christian Academy, the small Christian school my mom and our close friend Jenna, whom I called Aunt Nene, founded when I was in the fourth grade. Together, Jenna and my mom grew the university-model school every year, with my mom as the director. Students would attend class two to three days a week and spend the other days working at home with their parents. To this day, my mom continues to pour her heart and soul into the teachers and students of this precious school.

I slid into my seat right next to Sarah that September afternoon, excited for the start of the year. My day had been great so far. I'd caught up with my old friends and met new ones who had just entered our school. With fewer than one hundred students and around twenty teachers, newcomers were quite an event for us at Veritas. Following the university model, the school's classes were designed to be small, and they were especially so during the first few years of the school's existence. There were only twelve students in my class, and we all felt like family.

Bible class started at 1:00 in the afternoon that day, and we all sat excitedly waiting for our teacher's arrival. As he walked into the classroom, all eyes were on the tall man with the engaging smile. The moment he entered, I immediately felt an internal shift. It was as though he brought joy and light into the classroom with him, but I didn't understand why I felt that way.

Pastor Cameron McDonald gathered us around for introductions. He seemed kind and full of energy. As he asked each of us to introduce ourselves, he listened intently, which made us feel like we truly mattered to him. "What's your name, and what do you love most about this school?" Whatever our answer was, he responded like it was the best thing he'd heard all day.

After hearing about each student, Pastor Cameron then introduced himself, telling us about his family of six and the church where he was pastor. He also shared about a recent tragedy in his life. His brother-in-law—his best friend—had just died as the result of a car accident, leaving behind a wife and three young children. With the empathetic heart God put inside me, I felt his pain. My heart broke for this teacher I had just met.

But then Pastor Cameron began to share with us how much Jesus meant to him. That arrested my attention. Suddenly, he began to cry. This vivacious, strong man had big tears in his eyes at the mention of the name of Jesus, and that hit my heart with a wave of emotion and confusion. I had never seen anyone react that way to Jesus. I remember thinking, *This is a grown man, married with kids, and he's literally crying over the name of Jesus.* It was new and surprising to me, and it stirred something deep within my soul.

What I saw in him was beyond anything I had learned about before, and I wanted to know more. As though he knew my thoughts, he taught that day about knowing God and having a personal relationship with Him. Near the end of class, Pastor Cameron offered to pray over each of us individually. Being prayed over was nothing new to me, since my mom did it every night, but this time something happened inside me that I'd never experienced before.

"May I pray over you, Anne?" Pastor Cameron asked.

"Yes, please do," I responded.

"You are God's precious daughter," he said, looking intently at me. Then he began to pray. I wish I could remember the words of his prayer that day, but all I can remember are those sweet words he shared with me about how God sees me. And I remember how those words made me feel. I will never forget the liquid love that coursed through my veins and the powerful energy pulsing through my being. I didn't know what it was then, but I now know that feeling was the Holy Spirit. I felt love like a power source, in a way I'd never felt it before. I already knew what it was to be deeply loved by my parents. But this was different. This was life changing. This was power. And I wanted more of it.

If this grown man is crying over Jesus, I thought, *and I feel this kind of love, then everything I've learned about Jesus all my life must be real. Jesus must be real. It's true—all I've been taught, it's all true.*

Pastor Cameron ended our first Bible class together with worship unlike any I'd ever heard before. Instead of the hymns I was used to, he played a video of spontaneous worship with Steffany Gretzinger called "Tip of My Toes." I had never experienced worship music like this before, and it immediately drew me in. As I closed my eyes and began to worship God, another wave of the Holy Spirit hit my whole being. I may have looked calm on the outside, but on the inside, eternal transformation was beginning. I felt God pull me toward Him like a magnet. I knew He was real, and I wanted a personal relationship with Him. Everything I'd been taught as a kid suddenly connected inside me. All at once, my heart knew what my mind had always believed: *Not only is Jesus real, but He wants a relationship with me.*

Tears sprang to my eyes as I remembered the words I'd just heard about how God sees me: *precious daughter.* Undone by the depth of meaning in those two words, I whispered in my heart, *I am Your precious daughter. Thank You, Father.*

That night, alone in my room, I had the final sealing moment of this divine encounter. I went upstairs to be alone with God. Kneeling beside my bed, I bowed my head and let the tears come once again. "Jesus, thank You for dying for me and forgiving me of every bad thing I've ever done. I feel so free with You now, unashamed to stand in Your presence. I want You to be my Lord and my Savior both now and forever. I always want to feel this kind of love. I surrender to You completely." I went all in on Jesus because He had given all for me.

It's amazing how God weaves our moments together, such intricate little details that become the golden threads of our lives. He sees the end from the beginning, but we see only the moment. I relish the precious memories of my childhood—the imaginative play with my siblings, the love of my parents, the dream of going to space and exploring God's heavens—but at the time I only saw them as the regular moments of everyday life. I did not know that my heavenly Father was writing a story so much larger than my hopes to go to space or the sweet little adventures of my youth. He wove into me the very foundation I would need for the grander story *He* had in mind—one I didn't even know to dream.

A Note from Anne

As I was growing up, my parents made sure I had a rich understanding of who God is and what His Word says. Yet the transition from the head knowledge *about* God to the heart relationship *with* Him was a personal choice. It is the same for you. You may know as much as my childhood preacher does about God, but it's not until you've chosen to believe in Him with your *heart* that everything changes.

For me, that happened when I realized that all I had learned about God was true and I encountered Him as a person who *wanted* to have a relationship with me. All those times of watching the movie of Jesus' years on earth and seeing His interactions with people in their everyday lives suddenly became *real* to me. And on that first day of seventh grade, I experienced Him as Immanuel—"God with [me]." He is the God who enters real life with us and makes His presence known in everyday situations, because He *wants* a personal relationship with us. That is why the Son of God came, died, and rose again. Whether you've never known Him, only had a head knowledge of Him, or already walk in personal relationship with Him, I invite you into a deeper and more intimate relationship with Jesus right now. There is always more.

This is the word of faith that we preach: that if you confess with your mouth Jesus is Lord, and believe in your heart that God has raised Him from the dead, you will be saved.

ROMANS 10:8–9 MEV

TWO

Jacob Kent Wilson

When I was nine and Jacob was seventeen, my parents asked my brother to watch Liz and me overnight so they could take a quick trip to Cincinnati, about an hour and a half away. They didn't get the chance to go on dates very often, so this was a special treat.

My dad waited patiently by the door as Mom hugged us all for the third time and reminded Jacob of the rules. Finally, Daddy walked over and put his arm around Mom's waist. "Come on, sweetheart," he said. "If we don't leave now, we'll miss our reservation."

As they shut the door on their way out, I turned expectantly to Jacob. Anytime he was left in charge, something exciting was bound to happen. And true to form, Jacob winked at me and suggested I put on some clothes I could get wet.

Thirty minutes later, Liz and I stood waiting as Jacob pulled his two-person jon boat off his truck bed. We stepped forward to lift and shut the tailgate, trying our best to be helpers. Jacob dragged the boat down to the edge of the Kentucky River and motioned for us to join him. Liz and I squeezed together on the second seat as Jacob fired up the motor. We were off.

Jacob motored down the river for about twenty minutes while we girls chattered on about every little passing sight. We waved at other boats out on the water and tried to spot ducks swimming by. We were having the time of our lives. Then I had a brilliant idea.

"Let's FaceTime Mom and Daddy!" I said. "Jacob, can we, *please*?" After a moment of slight hesitation, Jacob handed over his phone. I was too excited for him to say no.

Liz and I huddled our heads together as we waited for Mom to answer the call.

When the call connected, I said, "Hey, Mom! Guess what we're doing?!"

"Oh my word, girls, where are you?" Mom's eyes grew round with worry.

"Jacob took us out on the river in the jon boat," I told her.

I could tell by her face that she was not happy, but before she could scold us, Jacob interrupted.

"Girls," he said, "the motor quit. Try to stay still while I fix it." Of course, Mom overheard every word and started to panic.

We stayed on the phone while Jacob tried to get the motor going, but he had no success. Finally, Daddy took the phone from Mom and told us to put Jacob on. Daddy gave him some advice about calling for help. I heard Jacob agree to do what he said and promise to call with an update. Then he ended the call. I was disappointed because I wasn't finished telling my mom all about our amazing adventure.

We floated for a few minutes until Jacob saw a boat nearby. He called out to the elderly couple in the boat, and they motored over to us.

"Y'all look like you might need some help," the man said.

"Yes, sir, we do," Jacob replied. "I got my sisters into a bit of a situation."

In short order, the gentleman and Jacob lifted us girls into the other boat and tied the jon boat behind it. They generously took us all the way back to Jacob's truck and even helped load the boat into the truck. As he drove us home, Jacob was probably thinking about the lecture Mom would give him when she returned, but all I thought about was how much I loved my trip in the boat with him. Too bad that motor had quit.

Boyhood Shenanigans

As a boy, Jacob gave my parents a run for their money. He had seemingly inexhaustible energy and the curiosity to match. My mom loves to tell stories of the phone calls she used to receive about Jacob.

"Hi, Lynn. I was just calling to make sure you knew that Jacob was out on your front lawn playing guitar . . . naked."

Sure enough, three-year-old Jacob, who was supposed to be napping, had made his way to the front yard, stripped down, and was giving a *memorable* performance for the neighborhood.

"Hello, Lynn? Did you know that Jacob is hanging out of a tree in your front yard, waving to all the kids going by on the school buses?"

True again. Like he often did, Jacob was doing his homeschool reading up in a tree. This time, instead of choosing his favorite tree in the backyard, he climbed a tree out front and cheerfully waved to all the kids on their way to school.

Some calls were more concerning. "Lynn!" Mom answered the phone to my uncle's angry voice. "I caught your boy red-handed, smoking a cigarette out on the farm!" When Daddy brought young Jacob home, Jacob's face was downcast.

"Why didn't you tell Daddy and me that you were curious about smoking?" Mom asked. "And where in the world did you get the idea to smoke a cigarette?"

"Mom," Jacob said, his eyes wide, "it's just that Mark Twain made it sound so good!"

Mom looked at Daddy, and they both did their best not to smile. Only Jacob would get an idea like that from his literature assignments.

My brother was also resourceful. By the time I was in first grade, Jacob had started attending the local high school. When I woke up one morning feeling nauseous, my mom decided I should stay home from our homeschool co-op since Jacob didn't have school that day. Mom left him with instructions before heading out to teach classes at the co-op.

A few hours later she called to check in and see how I was feeling. "Has Anne thrown up?" she asked. "Do you think she has a fever?"

"Oh no, Mom," Jacob said cheerfully. "She's doing great. I just fed her a big breakfast."

"What did she eat?" Mom asked, hoping the meal wouldn't make my stomach worse.

"Oh, I fed her some squirrel," Jacob said matter-of-factly.

"Squirrel?!" she exclaimed, then quickly lowered her voice. "Where did you get squirrel meat from?"

Killing and eating wild game wasn't unusual for Jacob, who had learned how to properly handle a gun and hunt from boyhood. But my mom knew there was no squirrel meat in the house. So where had Jacob gotten it? Turns out that when confronted with the need to feed his little sister breakfast, Jacob had found his own creative solution. He had gone up to his second-story bedroom, opened the window, and shot a squirrel out of a tree with his pellet gun. Downstairs, I heard a loud *pop* from my comfortable seat on the couch.

Jacob stowed away his pellet gun and ran down the stairs and outside to retrieve his prize. After skinning the poor critter in the kitchen sink, he prepared my breakfast: freshly cooked squirrel meat, served with powdered sugar on top and a side of BBQ dipping sauce. It was delicious!

The Best Big Brother

The summer I was ten, Jacob, who was eighteen at the time, helped bring to life my dream of a summer camp for children. For as long as I can remember, I have loved working with children.

My mom loves to tell a story from when I was two years old, when she would drop me off at the church nursery on Sunday mornings. She would quietly watch as I walked in and turned to greet the other toddlers as they arrived. I wasn't there to play. I was there to help. When my mom returned, she usually found me quietly rocking an infant, a look of pure contentment on my face.

The summer I started "Anne's Camp," I began with a few neighborhood children. Every day for a week, we met in my backyard from 10:00 to 3:00. I presented Bible stories, led art projects and games, and even taught science lessons. I charged my young campers a quarter for the week (but ended up reimbursing many of them who didn't want to part with their precious quarters).

The next summer I expanded Anne's Camp to include more neighborhood kids and family friends. By the time I was thirteen, Anne's Camp had grown to thirty kids, and getting ready for it was a family affair. Jacob helped me create a business plan and prepare for camp each year. He set up tables in the backyard and garage for our camp activities and built props for plays and science experiments. Elizabeth was able to take my theme for the year and design beautiful signs and whimsical snacks to go along with it. Mom was my right-hand woman, willing to help with any task I requested. Even Daddy chipped in where he could. Camp was a family event, and I was the ringleader.

The year following eighth grade, Anne's Camp grew large enough that I needed to move it from our home to Pastor Cameron's church. Since the day I had met him in seventh grade, I had become close friends with Pastor Cameron and his wife, Erica. I babysat their kids, and Erica had become a mentor to me. Both Cameron and Erica were spiritual leaders in my life. When Anne's Camp needed a larger venue, Pastor Cameron suggested I partner with their children's ministry to host it as the church's Vacation Bible School that year. We changed the name to Summer Spectacular Camp, and fifty children attended. Camp that year was official—complete with lanyards, schedules, volunteers, check-in, and waivers.

In August 2016, we were already planning Summer Spectacular Camp for the following summer. We expected 120 kids to attend the third week of June. I began to feel overwhelmed by the enormity of the task and wondered if I could pull it off.

One day, as we sat on the back patio, I voiced my doubts to Jacob. "I don't know," I said. "Maybe this is taking too much from our family. You'll be busy with college, and I don't think I can do it without your help. Do you think I should stop?"

"No, Annie!" he replied. "You can't give up now. These kids love your camp. I heard one of them say it was the best part of the whole summer." He shot me his killer smile. "Besides, you were born to do this."

Jacob leaned in for a hug and squeezed me tight. "I love to see you stepping into this gifting you have with such boldness," he said. He pulled back and grinned. "I'll still be around to help you. College classes don't last all year, you know."

Jacob was such an amazing big brother to Liz and me—our protector and our cheerleader. For Liz, he was also a childhood playmate, since they were closer in age. I love hearing about how they would dress up in camouflage clothes and put combat paint on their faces. With toy guns in hand, they'd play war for hours.

And when it came time for weekly piano lessons, Jacob used to put her on the handlebars of his bike and pedal them both down the street to our piano teacher's house. Mom made sure we all had piano lessons, whether we liked it or not.

Love of the Hunt

My brother loved pushing Liz and me out of our comfort zones. He wanted us to be competent *and* courageous. He was also passionate about hunting and fishing and included us as much as we would allow. One day Jacob brought the deer he had just killed to our Nana's house, which is near the family farm. Jacob called me out of Nana's house to help him field dress the deer.

"Hey, Annie," Jacob said, motioning toward the deer. "Hold this bag for me as I pull out the entrails. No big deal."

"*Ew,* Jacob. No!" I protested. "That's so gross!"

A smile tugged at the corners of his mouth, but his green eyes held a look of determination. "You can do it, Annie," he said. "You need to know how to do this. You can't let fear hold you back. Watch me and hold the bag steady."

I sighed, gazing at my brother's confident face. Then I grabbed the bag and turned toward the deer. Reluctantly, I held the bag open and watched Jacob's every move as he carefully cleaned out the deer. Being that close to the insides of a deer—seeing and smelling it—thoroughly grossed me out. But once we were done, I felt such a sense of accomplishment.

My brother was pleased too—both with himself and with me.

Since we were hunting together more frequently, he decided there should be one rule: "Any deer you kill, you have to skin and gut yourself," he told me.

I was not happy about this development. Though I offered to pay him to do it for me, he stuck to his rule. Let's just say I didn't hunt with him as much after that.

Luckily for Jacob, my dad was always game to join him hunting. Many fall days, Daddy and Jacob would put on their camouflage, load their equipment into the truck, and head out to the farm to hunt. They spent hours side by side, enjoying nature and each other. We didn't learn until much later that Daddy doesn't even enjoy hunting all that much. But he enjoyed Jacob with every fiber of his being, and he happily went hunting to be with his son.

Of all the hunting Jacob did, duck hunting was his true passion. He even chose his dog, Sallie, because of his love for the sport. A Boykin spaniel bred especially for duck hunting, Sallie was his constant companion while hunting and at home. Mom, Liz, and I sometimes worried about Sallie because Jacob would take her out hunting on extremely cold days.

He and his buddies chose the coldest days possible to hunt ducks because that's when the birds huddle together in groups to conserve energy. By the end of a successful hunt, sweet little Sallie would sometimes have icicles hanging from her ears and nose. But Jacob watched her closely and knew just when to run her back to the truck to warm up. They had a special bond. Boykin spaniels attach to just one person and are extremely loyal, often becoming stressed when separated from that individual. Jacob was Sallie's person.

A Helping Hand

One January day, Jacob went duck hunting with his friend Dan and Dan's brother, Jack. The guys had been watching the weather for weeks to find the coldest day of the season to get out on the Kentucky River. That day happened to be the same day Dan had to catch a ride back to the Citadel, a military college in South Carolina. Winter break was ending, and the guys decided to take one last hunting trip before returning to classes—Dan at the Citadel and Jacob at the University of Kentucky. Though they had started their college careers together at the Citadel, Jacob now attended UK so he could be closer to home.

They decided to head out on their hunting trip but knew they would have to watch their time so Dan didn't miss his ride. They got about five miles downriver in the boat, realized they were running late, and decided to fire up the motor and head back to the truck. The motor had other ideas. The low temperatures had made it impossible to start. Jacob tried everything he knew to do for about thirty minutes before finally giving up.

Dan didn't want to miss his ride, so he decided to walk back. Jacob joined him, assuring Jack he'd drive the truck back for him and the gear. That walk was much longer and colder than either of them expected, and they were soon chilled and miserable. Finally, they spotted the truck across a creek that was fifteen feet across. The creek was covered by a thin layer of ice, but the ice was not nearly thick enough to hold their weight. In hopes of crossing the creek without getting wet, they searched the bank for a fallen tree to lay across it, but to no avail.

"Buddy, if you're going to catch your ride, I think we're going to have to swim across," Jacob said. He was right—it was the only way. The two men stripped off their outer layers, slid their clothing and boots across the thin ice, and stood at the edge.

"You ready?" Jacob asked, looking at his friend.

"Ready as I'll ever be," Dan answered.

They plunged into the icy water. They had to swim out and around the ice, so the distance was about thirty feet. Halfway to shore, Dan realized no matter how hard he tried, he wasn't making progress. His strokes became slower, and his head dipped beneath the icy water. Dan inhaled some water and began to panic. He slowly started to sink.

At that exact moment, Jacob reached a tree branch and turned to see his friend fighting for his life. Holding onto the branch with one hand, Jacob reached his other arm back to grasp Dan's arm, just in time. Jacob pulled Dan over to the tree where Dan was able to grab hold of the branch and catch his breath. Then Jacob wrapped an arm under Dan's arms and around his chest and pulled him the final fifteen feet to shore.

Dan would later say that if he'd been on his own that day, he wouldn't have survived. It was such a traumatic moment for him, he's had nightmares about it since. He knows if it weren't for God's divine protection through Jacob, he would have died that day.

I was overjoyed that Jacob had returned to Lexington to attend UK for his sophomore year. That meant a return to Sunday dinners, trips to the farm, and watching basketball together. In our state, UK basketball is a way of life. And like most people who live here, the Wilsons bleed blue. When Jacob was a student at UK, I loved it when he would invite me to attend a home game with him. I felt so mature standing in the student section and cheering till my throat hurt.

Before the game, Daddy would drive me downtown to meet Jacob a few hours before tipoff. Decked out in our blue and white, Jacob and I would walk about a mile to get to Rupp Arena. During that time, Jacob often gave me one of his famous lectures, imparting bits and pieces of wisdom.

One afternoon, we walked along the streets of Lexington with a crowd of fans all flowing in the same direction. At a crosswalk, while we all waited to cross, someone spoke rudely to me.

"Jacob!" I said. "Did you hear what he said to me? I have a mind to tell him he needs to learn some manners."

"No, Annie," Jacob said. "Don't do that. Never burn bridges."

"You always say that," I replied. "Never burn bridges—but why? I'll never see him again."

"Listen," Jacob said after we'd crossed the intersection. "You never know what someone else is going through. And God doesn't call us to judge. Plus, who knows? That guy might save your life someday!"

I looked at Jacob incredulously but simply said, "Okay." There was no use arguing. I'd never change my brother's mind. Jacob didn't let anyone talk negatively about others in his presence.

We continued walking as Jacob positioned me next to him, away from the street. "Let me tell you something else, Annie," he said. "Don't you ever date a guy who lets you walk next to the curb. A gentleman should always put himself between you and the road."

The Last Lecture

The last lecture I received from Jacob happened in the late spring of 2017. He was twenty-three and I was fourteen. By this time, Jacob had his own apartment in town, but he still stopped by the house for family dinners and to hang out. That evening, Jacob called me into the family room. He told me he wanted to share something important with me. Knowing a lecture was imminent, I nestled into the couch and prepared to be there awhile.

I looked up at my brother expectantly. Jacob stood tall and handsome, looking down at me with his shining green eyes. His dark hair swayed slightly as he spoke to me, his deep voice full of kindness.

That day, I was eager to hear his words and captivated by his care for me. On other occasions, I'd been too immature to appreciate his advice and couldn't wait for his lectures to be over. But this time, I listened.

I believe that what happened that night was God's gift to me. God gave me the ability to appreciate Jacob's desire to help me. If God hadn't given me that capability, I'd feel a deep regret for tuning out Jacob's final lecture.

You probably wonder what that last lecture was about. Me too. I know it sounds odd that I can't remember, but it's true. I simply don't recall the specifics of our talk. Perhaps the memory loss is due to trauma's effect on my brain. But what matters most is that Jacob and I connected that day. I think God knew I needed to remember that moment with my brother more than I needed to recall his actual advice. Certainly, the Lord knew just how much I would treasure that memory in the days to come.

A Note from Anne

Jacob could always see the best in every situation or person. Even on a bad day, he somehow found something to be grateful for or happy about. Because he carried this attitude with him through life, he was almost always joyful, and his joy was contagious. He was the one who could cheer up our family when we were sad or in conflict. He was the one who helped me learn to speak positive words toward others.

I think his grateful heart—the kind that could see the best in things—is why he loved life so much and why others so deeply loved him. Gratefulness kept him from a sense of entitlement and helped him find strength in hard times. Whole books can be and have been written about being grateful and positive. I won't attempt that here. I'll just say that Jacob was the living textbook that I studied for so many years, and he taught me the importance of giving thanks in all circumstances and expressing the joy of the Lord. I still struggle to do those things and wonder how he did them so well. If I could share with you one lesson I learned from Jacob, it would be to keep your heart in a position of gratitude and watch for the many things in life that bring joy. Jacob always did, and we can too.

> Rejoice always. Pray without ceasing. In everything give thanks, for this is the will of God in Christ Jesus concerning you.
>
> 1 Thessalonians 5:16–18 MEV

THREE

June 7, 2017

Tuesday, June 6, 2017, was a gorgeous, sunny day. That evening Mom, Elizabeth, and I had dinner with Aunt Nene and her daughters, Emma and Sarah, on the patio of our favorite restaurant. The soft evening light illuminated our faces as we talked and laughed, and everything seemed right with the world. On our way home, we stopped by the store for Liz to grab a few things. While Mom and I waited in the car, she called Jacob to remind him of a dental appointment later that week. His phone went straight to voice mail, so she left him a message, closing with her usual "I love you!"

"I guess he let his phone die again," she said, ending the call. That was nothing unusual, and none of us gave it a second thought.

Originally, Jacob was planning to go golfing with Daddy that evening, but he changed plans at the last minute, deciding to join his girlfriend for dinner at Hall's on the River, his favorite special-event restaurant. They were celebrating her passing her final nursing exam.

Daddy didn't mind the change of plans. Golfing was his and Jacob's thing—they loved to get on the green together—and there would be plenty of other times to golf. So that night, Jacob spent the evening on the deck of this nostalgic tavern, eating fresh catfish while gazing out on his beloved Kentucky River.

Late that evening, I was on the phone with a good friend from school discussing our upcoming sophomore year and all the things we wanted to do before summer's end, including Summer Spectacular Camp. I was excited because it would be our biggest camp yet and was only weeks away. Just after midnight, we talked about Jacob and how he had been helping me plan the setup for camp.

I had seen Jacob the night before when he'd come over for dinner. On his way out, he'd stopped by my room to say goodbye.

"Hey, Annie, I'm leaving," he said, popping his head through the doorway. I was bent over my plans for our camp.

"Bye!" I said. I lifted my head slightly to smile at Jacob, but I didn't hop up to hug him like I usually would. I was so engrossed in my plans that I let him leave without a hug.

Mom and Elizabeth are night owls and love to stay up collaborating, even after I've hit my limit. They were up until 2:00 a.m. working on Liz's artistic contributions to my camp. Daddy had slipped off to bed earlier in the evening, needing to be up early for work. After talking with my friend, I turned in a little before 1:00.

"Anne! Wake up, Anne!" Elizabeth's frantic voice jarred me

from sleep. "Something is wrong! I think something might be wrong with Jacob!" My phone told me it was a little after 3:00 a.m., and my mind began to spin, remembering that our neighborhood had experienced some recent robberies. Maybe someone was trying to break in.

Liz can't see anything without her contacts or glasses, so I rose quickly to look out my bedroom window. On the street in front of our house, I saw flashing red and blue lights—lots of them.

I still remember what I was wearing in that moment—shorts with little green four-leaf clovers on them and a white T-shirt. Still in my pajamas, I rushed down the stairs, and when I reached the foot, I froze. Six police officers stood in a line in our entryway, their backs against the front door, hands crossed in front of them. I heard cries coming from the other room, but I couldn't take my eyes off the police officers. When I saw their sorrowful expressions, a deep fear gripped me.

"What is going on?" I said. "Please tell me what is happening!"

But they didn't. They stood calm and composed, but I saw pity in their eyes. I turned my attention to gut-wrenching screams coming from the living room. I will never forget the devastation that met my gaze.

My strong, beautiful mama sat crumpled in a chair crying, screaming, and clenching her fists. I felt physically ill seeing her like this.

Something must be terribly wrong with Jacob, I thought as my breath caught in my throat. *He must be in some major trouble.* As I continued to survey the room, it felt as though time had slowed. There was Daddy, sitting on the couch weeping with his head in his hands. I had never seen my Daddy, the rock of our family, weep before, and it shook me to my core.

That's when I knew. Daddy would only cry like that over one of his kids.

"Daddy, is it Jacob?" I dared ask. "Is he dead?"

He raised his head and his vacant eyes met mine. "Yeah, Anne." His tone dripped with angry disbelief. "He's dead."

Everything seemed to stop as my dad's words ricocheted in my mind. *He's dead.*

I could barely catch my breath as my mind reeled with this impossible information. I felt my body go cold as I stood utterly still, unable to move. *No! This* cannot *be true,* I thought. *I just saw Jacob last night.*

God's Voice in the Dark

As the unbelievable knowledge of my brother's death bombarded my being, God's voice filled my mind. For the first time in my life, I heard God audibly speak to me.

Anne, are you going to trust Me, or are you not?

The voice was commanding yet gentle. Even though I'd never heard God speak to me in this way, I instantly knew it was His voice. I also had a keen awareness that He wasn't going to be upset with me if my answer was no. He would not be mad if I didn't trust Him. This encounter was His firm yet kind way of making me choose what I would do—where my trust would be—from the very first moment of my grief.

I turned away from my dad and gazed across the front hall into the family room, where my eyes landed on a portrait of Jacob, Elizabeth, and me happily smiling into the camera.

"Jesus, I trust You," I whispered.

Those were the first words that left my lips after I learned of my brother's death. *Jesus, I trust You.* That utterance was the first of many miracles to follow. As soon as the words left my lips, a sense of heaviness lifted. I was still in shock—still numb and sick with grief—but somehow, I felt lighter. Then He spoke again.

I'm going to give you everything you need to push through this tragedy.

I sensed God filling my being with His words. And I believed Him. I knew I was facing something harder than I'd ever experienced before, but I was sure He would help me through it.

I turned to speak to the man standing nearest to me, the deputy coroner. "Please," I pleaded, "tell me what happened to my brother."

"He was in a car accident," the man said. "We are so sorry for your loss." Then he reached out and placed in my hands a bag of Jacob's things—the items that had been on him when he died. The plastic bag contained his work ID, his wallet, and his receipts from dinner.

These ordinary objects made the news all too real. *These things should be with Jacob, not here with me.* I gazed down at Jacob's work ID in my hands, and his smiling face looked up at me. The image of him popping his head through my door to say goodbye the night before flashed through my mind. *He was here just yesterday. How can he be gone? How am I holding his belongings?*

At that moment, Elizabeth came running down the stairs. What felt like an eternity had only been a few minutes, during which Elizabeth had put in her contacts. She began asking the same frantic questions. I saw the same terrified look in her eyes that had been in mine just moments before.

"What's going on?" she cried. "What's wrong?" I heard the desperation in her voice as she took in the scene before her. Her eyes landed on me. No one else was speaking, so I finally told her the horrible news.

"Jacob's dead." I spoke out loud the worst words I've ever uttered.

Liz gasped for breath and began to hyperventilate. I reached out to help my sister as her body locked up. She couldn't process such horrifying news. None of us could. When I heard myself say those awful words, it felt like my insides were ripping apart. I knew Liz must be feeling the same. Time slowed and our senses failed. The pain threatened to destroy us. We all had different outward reactions to the inner wreckage—screaming, weeping, hyperventilating, stillness—but each of us was leveled by the grief.

I was the still one. I looked on in silence, listening, but not hearing. Watching, but not really seeing. My body revolted against this new reality. *It just can't be. Jacob can't be gone.*

I don't know how long the police officers and coroner stayed. It felt like a long time, but it might have only been a few minutes. They did what they could to console us and answer our questions. The police officers explained to my parents how and where Jacob's truck had hit a light pole as he drove home. He had died instantly, just after midnight on June 7. Even with that information, my mom could not accept the reality that her son was gone.

"This isn't true!" she kept repeating. "Where is he? Where's Jacob? I need to see my son!"

"We're sorry for your loss, ma'am," the deputy coroner said. "We're so sorry."

Although the officers seemed reluctant to leave us in our desperate state, there was nothing more for them to do. With shoulders drooped and eyes reflecting our consuming pain, they turned and walked out. As the door shut behind them, we were left there, barely able to breathe, surrounded by the darkness of night and the darkness of death. I did the only thing I knew to do.

"We need to pray," I said, gathering the four of us together in the kitchen. I don't know why those were the first words I spoke to my grieving family or why I was the strong one in that moment; I was just as shocked and grief-stricken as they were. But God had spoken to me and lifted a heaviness off me. He was giving me direction one step at a time. I know it came from Him—the direction, the strength, the words. All of it.

"God, thank You for the twenty-three years You gave us Jacob," I prayed. "Thank You for the twenty-three years we had with him." I don't remember the rest of my words, but I remember those. *Give thanks in all things.* I never could have done that in my own strength. It all came from Him. In that moment, I realized we could try to survive this in our own strength or we could turn to the One—the only One—who could get us through it. I knew I could never endure this without God, so I wasn't angry with Him. Instead, I clung to Him; He was all I had.

After praying, we went upstairs to our rooms in a daze. None of us had any idea what to do next. When I walked into my room, my eyes focused on the pile of laundry I had folded earlier that evening. Doing the laundry is my job in our household, so that pile was a commonplace sight. As I stared at the neatly folded clothes, a surreal thought filled my brain: *Who would have known that six hours after folding these clothes my brother would be dead?* Our minds protect us from what is too much to bear, and that was happening for me. I felt numb and disconnected, noticing odd little details around me.

Jacob had left us that night just after midnight. Literally seconds after he left this earth, I had been casually conversing with my friend. We spoke of Jacob as though he were still with us, but he wasn't. He had just died in a car crash on his way back to his apartment. Jacob immediately joined Jesus, yet we had no idea he was gone.

I walked over to my parents' bedroom and saw them in their agony. Maybe someday, when I'm a parent, I'll understand a tiny fraction of what they have suffered in losing their baby boy. They were hugging each other tightly. As the pain overwhelmed her, my mom began to rip my dad's shirt, not even realizing what she was doing. The pain was too great to be contained in her little body.

"Mom," I offered gently, taking a step toward them, "remember what you've always told us kids—that we are only on loan to you from God." Mom turned to look at me and then reached out to draw me into their embrace. As we stood there together, I wondered at the words I had just spoken. I don't know how I knew to say that or how it impacted my mom, but it just came out. As excruciating as that statement was, it was true.

Visions of Jesus

By the grace of God, despite my shell-shocked state, I knew I needed to call Pastor Cameron next. I'd recently been attending the youth group at his church and occasionally visiting on Sunday mornings. Because I looked to Pastor Cameron and Erica as mentors, I knew I needed their support. As I pulled out my phone, my dad leaned against the wall and melted to the floor, tears streaming down his face. The phone rang and rang. Of course, Pastor Cameron was asleep at such an hour. I tried again. And again.

When he finally answered, I broke down. Through my sobs, I managed to say, "My brother is dead."

"No, no, no, no," Pastor Cameron said. "It can't be. No, no, it just can't be." He told me later that my call had given him flashbacks to losing his own brother-in-law and best friend. "I'll be right there."

I didn't have to say anything else. Twenty minutes later, Pastor Cameron walked through the door. He was the first person we told and the first to come. He entered our devastation with us, knowing firsthand the pain of losing someone you care for so deeply. He sat with my mom on the couch and began to weep with her and pray with her.

"I need to know where he is!" my mom cried. "Where is Jacob

right now? What is he doing?" She was desperate to know something, anything about her son who had been ripped from her.

"Lynn, on my drive here, as I prayed for you, God showed me a vision of Jacob," Pastor Cameron said. "He was wrapped up in the arms of the Father. That is where he is *right now*—in the arms of the Father." My mom breathed a little easier, picturing her son encircled by the arms of God. You could see her body relax and peace come over her. Cameron went on to say he felt in his spirit that God would not waste this tragedy and would bring something incredibly beautiful from these ashes.

Ashes. What an apt word. The aftermath of a tragedy is like the ash and debris after a terrible explosion—everything you knew is gone, and you are surrounded by destruction. Your senses don't work right, your mind cannot comprehend any of it, and you don't feel like you can even take your next breath. You wander aimlessly until you get hit by another excruciating wave of pain—the kind that is so strong you feel like you will literally die from it. And sometimes, you just wish you would, so the agony would end.

But in the ashes of our lives, God met us. He sent us loved ones to be His voice, His arms, His comfort, His presence. We called, and they came. My mom's brother was the second one to arrive. As soon as he walked through the door, he began sharing Scripture with us to keep our minds focused on the Lord.

From 4:30 until 8:00 a.m., Elizabeth and I made the calls no one ever wants to make or receive. We called Jacob's roommate Ben, Chuck and Dan and Jacob's other friends, his girlfriend, and many others. I called a few of my friends from school. We called Aunt Nene, Emma, and Sarah, who are like family to us, and it was just as awful to tell them about Jacob as it was to tell our extended family members. When my mom's sister, Aunt Bebe, found out, she immediately began the drive from Missouri.

The sun finally rose a little after 6:00 a.m. We needed the sunrise that morning more than we'd ever needed it before. Once the sun was up, Daddy called his sister so she could go be with his mom when she heard the news of Jacob's death.

After we made the initial calls, a strong desire—more like a need—rose up in me. I felt like I needed to speak to Kelsey, a young lady from Pastor Cameron's church. I knew her from my frequent visits to their church, and I looked up to her as an example of someone who follows Jesus well. She had also gone to the same high school as Jacob for a while, so she had a connection to our family. Still, I didn't know why I felt such a pressing urge to talk to her right then. All I knew was that I could not shake the feeling.

I asked Pastor Cameron if he would ask her to call me, and a short time later my phone rang. I walked out onto the patio to speak with her alone. The first sound I heard when I picked up was Kelsey weeping. Pastor Cameron had already told her that Jacob was gone, and she just cried with me for a few moments. I told her that I had felt an urgency to speak with her right away. And as our conversation unfolded, the reason became obvious—God began to give her visions of my family.

"I see you, Anne," she said quietly. "I see you, and Jesus is kneeling in front of you. He's holding your face and wiping your tears away. Anne, Jesus is weeping with you." I could not see what she saw in the Spirit, but I felt it. As my tears flowed, I felt the nearness of Jesus, as though we were locked together, eye to eye.

And I knew that He was with me right then and there—weeping with me.

"I see your sister, Elizabeth, standing in the same place as you," Kelsey went on. "She, too, is weeping. Jesus is kneeling before her, and He is weeping. Her face is turned away from Him, and He is gently turning her face to look into His." This was also true. Jesus had already turned my face toward His, and our eyes were locked. But Elizabeth had not yet turned to Him. She was not mad at Him, but she was not yet looking to Him as her source of strength. Like Martha and Mary in the Bible when they lost their beloved brother, Lazarus, I ran to Jesus immediately like Martha, and like Mary, Liz stayed hidden away. Though our pace was different, we would both get to Jesus eventually, which was what mattered.

"I see your mom, Anne," Kelsey continued. "And she is in God's lap. He is squeezing her so tightly, holding her close, and saying, 'It's going to be okay.'" This was the truest thing she could have said. My mom was so devastated she *needed* to be held by God, wrapped up in His arms like a little child. And God was showing me He was doing exactly that.

"And I see your dad," Kelsey said. "He is standing up straight. He looks strong, but God is holding him up from behind." My sweet daddy was trying so hard to be strong for all of us, yet part of him just wanted to give up. Kelsey's words confirmed that God would not let him go—He was holding on tightly, strong arms around my daddy, providing the strength he needed.

Kelsey's visions gave me deep comfort. Each so perfectly captured where each of us was right then, in our fresh grief. Every picture showed me how God was tenderly caring for us in just the way we needed. He had shown Pastor Cameron that Jacob was in His arms. And He had shown Kelsey that each of us was also being held and comforted by Him. I knew Jesus was with us in the pain. He sat with us. He held us. He wept with us. He counted our many tears. He was right in the middle of our grief. Psalm 56:8 says, "You keep track of all my sorrows. You have collected all my tears in your bottle. You have recorded each one in your book" (NLT). Those words became reality to me.

At the end of our conversation, Kelsey prayed a beautiful prayer for me and told me to call her anytime. With a new level of peace in my heart, I ended the call and turned back to rejoin my family. *Remember He's right with you,* I told myself. *Jesus has promised to carry you through.* I took a deep breath and walked back into the house.

God's Comforters

I remember the comforters God sent to us that day. On a day like that, when your world changes forever, you remember who God sends to comfort you. And God sent just the right people to sit with us in the ashes of our grief.

My parents' friends came and held them as they cried. My mom's friends brought such perfect comforts—essential oil diffusers that flooded our home with soothing aromas and sticky notes with scriptures written on them to place around our home. Many times, in the days to come, we'd pick up those sticky notes and read a verse that was just the right word at the right time. God sent many friends who were like family to Liz and me, and they joined us in our grief. Jacob had been like a brother to them. Pastors, old and new, came to minister to us. And of course, the family came. Some family members whom we had not seen in a long time came; even from the first moment, God began to bring restoration out of the tragedy.

My mom's friends—incredible women of faith—showed up first thing that morning and sat with her during her moments of deepest despair. When the finality of her son's death took her to a dark place and thoughts of Jacob's suffering during his final moments on earth threatened to destroy her, these precious women collected photographs of Jacob from around the house and laid them in my mother's lap as she cried and clenched her fists.

"Tell us, Lynn," her friends invited. "Tell us about Jacob. Tell us stories about your son." And she did. One by one, she picked up the frames, held them to her heart, and told of her beautiful boy.

Her eyes fell on a photograph of Jacob with his Little League baseball team. "That team won the state championship when he was ten," she said. "But the highlight for Jacob wasn't winning the game but finding a snake. He and his friend, Chuck, found it in a nearby creek before the game. Oh, the people they scared with that snake!" A hint of a smile played at the corners of her mouth.

"My sweet boy, so full of life . . . ." Her voice trailed off into sobs.

Her friends encircled her, loving her with all they had, listening to her tell the stories of Jacob. Her tears fell until the frames were drenched, and her friends wept with her, fulfilling the words of Romans 12:15 to "weep with those who weep" (NLT). Thank God they did. Those moments were the first I saw my mom smile since learning of Jacob's death. The presence of those friends pulled her from the edge of despair and led her to a brighter place of happy memories and loving feelings for Jacob. She couldn't rise from the deep sadness on her own, so God sent these beautiful souls to help her.

Even with such deep pain covering my family that day, I still saw God's touches of grace and comfort through it all. I had heard His audible voice for the first time in my life. When asked to trust Him, by some miracle, I had said yes. He had turned my face toward His and joined me in my sorrow, counting every tear. He had even sent precious friends to sit with us in the darkest hours of our lives.

That night, as I lay on the mattress I had dragged into my parents' bedroom, I reflected on how my life had changed forever in a single moment. It would never be the same again. *I* would never be the same again. I didn't know how I could endure another day of this pain, let alone a lifetime without Jacob. I closed my eyes, longing for the sweet relief of sleep. As I drifted off, I remembered again God's promise to me that day to give us everything we needed to survive this tragedy. Once again, I chose to believe Him and whispered my words of surrender: *Jesus, I trust You.*

A Note from Anne

God is real, and God is good. When I experienced the worst day of my life, these were the foundational truths I clung to. From the beginning, Satan tried to convince Eve that God was not good, and he still tries to slip us the same lie in our times of loss. When our hearts are ripped open in pain, the Enemy of our souls shoots his fiery arrows and tries to convince us that God does not have our best interests at heart and that He's not good. It can be easy to believe these lies, not only because we are vulnerable but also because our experiences seem to agree.

But more real than the Enemy's whispered lies is the reality that God draws near to our shattered hearts. In His goodness, He enters our pain. I've heard it said, "What if the point of Job wasn't *why* God allows suffering, but *how* God is present in our suffering?" At the worst moment of my life, God spoke to me and asked me to trust Him; He promised to help me through it. He did not turn His back on me. He came in even closer. In the days that followed, He did the same for each member of my family. Safety and healing are found in trusting in God's character and His Word. No wonder the Enemy tries so hard to keep us from it.

> The righteous cry out, and the Lord hears,
> and delivers them out of all their troubles.
> The Lord is near to the broken-hearted,
> and saves the contrite of spirit.
>
> Psalm 34:17–18 MEV

FOUR

Choosing to Trust

"No one ever told me that grief felt so like fear. I am not afraid, but the sensation is like being afraid," wrote C. S. Lewis, the great author and apologist, in *A Grief Observed* after losing his beloved wife, Joy. It's true. Grief does feel like fear.

In the days immediately following Jacob's death, this sensation of fear gripped my insides, turning my stomach into a churning pit day and night. When the panic arose, my mind raced. I shook. I couldn't get warm. I struggled to breathe or even swallow. I ached all the way to my bones.

The sorrow built up inside until I felt like my body could not hold another ounce of agonizing grief. But I was wrong—there was more. I'm thankful that the most intense moments of grief come in waves, and between each one I had a chance to regain my footing before getting swept under again. If not for that mercy, I think I might have died from it.

The morning of Thursday, June 8, I awoke to the deepest

sorrow I had ever known. We were barely twenty-four hours past hearing the news about Jacob, and Dad, Mom, Liz, and I had spent the first dark night together in my parents' bedroom where Liz and I had pulled our mattresses onto the floor. We couldn't bear to be separated. I didn't want to be alone for a single second, so we stayed together. The next morning, we rose from our beds to face a day that never should have existed. It all felt so unnatural.

When I was young, I often had nightmares. I remember the relief I felt upon waking and realizing it was "only a dream." After losing Jacob, our mornings became the exact opposite. We woke up to the nightmare and wished our dreams were reality instead.

That first morning of waking up to "the after" is hard to describe. Yes, we felt intense pain at the fresh realization of losing Jacob, but at the same time we felt numb. We moved like robots as we went through the motions of our daily routines, dressing almost without thinking. To a casual observer we may have looked normal, but nothing about us was normal.

None of us felt a desire to eat. In fact, I felt physically incapable of doing so, like my body was giving up. I felt no hunger or thirst. Making decisions was nearly impossible—especially for my mom. The trauma of being violently robbed of her son affected her brain not only that day but for many months to come.

We knew we had to see to Jacob's truck and retrieve his belongings. The four of us piled into the car, and Daddy drove us to the towing company. My mom turned on the radio to fill the silence. But as soon as she hit the button, the words of "Even If" by MercyMe filled the car. We sat in stunned silence, listening to lyrics that suddenly held new meaning for us. They declared hope in God amid a fiery trial. It was as though the lyrics had been written just for us.

The song confronted us with a weighty question: Would we trust God, even if or when the worst had happened? We looked at each other as the last notes of the song dissipated. My mom reached to turn off the radio. Then she asked the question we were all thinking.

"Are we going to turn our backs on God?" she said, her facial muscles tensed in pain. "Or are we going to trust that He is good *even if* we've lost Jacob?"

Daddy shook his head. "We won't turn our backs on Him. I may not be ready to talk to Him yet, but this family won't turn from God." We all nodded in agreement. Whether or not we felt it, we made a choice that morning—we would believe in the goodness of God even when the worst had happened.

I wish I could forget our experience at the towing company, but it is forever seared in my memory. Elizabeth and I waited in the car. My parents didn't want us to see Jacob's mangled truck. Liz was fine with that, but I was longing for closure and thought seeing the truck might offer it. I think it's for the best I didn't go, though. When my parents crossed to the other side of the thick wooden fence, where the truck was, Liz and I heard our mother's bloodcurdling scream through both the fence and the closed car windows. Dad later told us that when she saw the truck, she collapsed onto his chest. When they eventually returned to the car, Daddy gently helped Mom back into her seat because she had no strength left.

From the back seat, I watched my mom weep and clench her

fists. For months to follow, she would continue to clench her fists to cope with her overwhelming emotions.

After leaving the towing company, we drove to the scene of the accident to visit the place where Jacob had died. There were still fresh tire marks and oil stains on the street where the crash had occurred, intensifying the grief and horror we felt. We later learned that a police officer was sitting at the same intersection and saw the accident happen. Jacob drove through a yellow light at the same moment another car drove into the intersection. In a split-second decision, Jacob jerked his wheel to avoid being broadsided but instead drove directly into an electrical pole. The officer ran to help, but Jacob was already in the presence of Jesus.

Standing there, my mom surveyed the scene and a nearby preschool and fire station, then mumbled quietly, "I used to teach at that preschool and walk my little students to the park right past this intersection. Who knew then that this is where my son would die?" She began to sob, remembering how she had taken Jacob to that very fire station when he was a little boy and dreamed of being a fireman.

Reminders of Jacob

That day Uncle Pete, Aunt Bebe's husband, arrived and accompanied us to Jacob's apartment. Inside, I slowly looked around, but my mind struggled to comprehend that Jacob wasn't there. I saw items so recently touched by him—his jacket slung over the back of his chair, the hunting gear hanging in the closet, his toothbrush and cologne on the bathroom counter. He had just been here. I picked up his cologne and twisted off the cap. My brother's familiar scent filled my nostrils, and I couldn't stop the tears. I squeezed my eyes shut and could see Jacob before me, so full of life. *He can't be gone!* My mind struggled to accept reality. Surely, he'd walk in that door any minute.

I replaced the cap on the bottle of cologne and put it in a box. The tears continued to stream down my face as I added some of his duck calls and favorite hats to the box. As I packed up my brother's belongings, something shifted in me. He wasn't coming back. It wasn't the closure I was searching for, but it did feel like a door in my heart was shutting. Jacob was gone, and so was my childhood. I could never go back.

My mother could not stop weeping as she held to her chest one precious item after another. Occasionally, she would have to stop and catch her breath while my dad came and wrapped his arms around her. His own grief was overwhelming, but somehow he found the strength to support my mom.

We brought away all that we could bear to take that day. My uncle would collect the rest the following week.

Later that same day, my mom and I walked together into Jacob's old bedroom at home. On that bed, I'd had many long talks with my big brother. From the window directly before me, he'd shot the squirrel for my breakfast. The memories of Jacob in that room both drew us to it and made us scared to enter. We wanted to feel close to him, but the memories were overwhelming in the most excruciating way. I still struggled to accept he was really gone. *He stayed in this room when he spent the night for Christmas,* I thought. *I just know he will again. This is wrong. All of this is wrong.* Though his things were there, my brother was gone.

"Anne, his belt!" My mother's whispered words broke into my thoughts. "I never finished the needlepoint belt for Jacob."

When my mom and dad were newly married, my mom had needlepointed several special items for Daddy, including an ornate belt. A few years earlier, Jacob had asked Mom to make him a needlepoint belt like the one she'd made for Daddy. The project was intricate and required a lot of time and patience to complete. My mom had been so busy being a wife and mother and directing our school that she had not completed Jacob's belt. Now he was gone, and I could see by her tears that she agonized over what she had failed to do for her son.

"Mom," I said gently. "Look at all the things you gave Jacob that are still here in his room. See this shirt you just got him on vacation? See his baseball trophies? Look at that deerskin rug you helped him make from his first deer. He couldn't take any of this with him. He's in heaven where none of it matters now."

I paused, watching my mother process all I was saying. Then I continued. "But the character and the love of God that you instilled in him, that still matters. He took those things with him, Mom." Mom nodded her head and reached out to embrace me.

That first week, family and friends visited us constantly. They brought us food in abundance and handled any tasks we assigned them. Most importantly, they were simply *there.* That was a great help to me, as I did not want to be alone, even to sleep. I asked my friends to stay with me every waking moment. Emma and Sarah, who had seldom left our sides as little girls, stayed by us during our darkest days. They, too, grieved the loss of Jacob, who was like a brother to them. Sarah, who is my age, even spent the night with me so I didn't have to be alone.

Liz, on the other hand, wanted to be left alone. She locked herself in her room and only spoke to family and a few close friends. The first week, mornings were unbearable for Liz. We all awoke to the nightmare of losing Jacob, but she relived the trauma to a greater extent. She continued to wake each morning, groggy and thinking it was all a dream. And each morning, she had to realize that it wasn't just a dream and Jacob was really gone.

God's Comfort

Two days after Jacob's accident, Pastor Cameron's sister, Ashley, came to visit with us at my request. I knew her through Pastor Cameron's family and visits to their church. She brought her son Lane with her, who was around my age. Ashley had a unique understanding of our grief, having lost her husband and the father of her three children a few years earlier from a horrible car accident.

"Oh, Anne." Ashley reached for me as she walked through the door. Her arms wrapped around me, and I relaxed into her embrace. She knew.

"Ashley, thank you for coming," I said. "I needed to see you." I let out a sob. "I need to know I can survive this."

"You will survive this," she said. She and Lane sat with Mom and me in the family room. Daddy and Liz had retreated to their bedrooms, but we heard an occasional wail drift down the stairs from Liz's room.

"I know the despair you are feeling right now," Ashley said gently. "And it's hard to imagine it will ever get better. You can't imagine even giving a genuine smile ever again in this lifetime, can you?"

I nodded, letting out a soft sob.

"But you will," she continued. "God will carry you through. His Holy Spirit will minister to you in deep places, and you will be blessed from it. You'll see—He's more faithful than you ever knew."

I believed her words because she had so recently walked this same path. She knew what the first few days—and first few months—felt like. Ashley offered us the hope of someone who had survived.

Lane sat by his mother's side with a compassionate look on his face. I could tell he understood my agony. Ashley turned to him and nodded, encouraging him to share from his own experience.

"It's true, Anne," Lane said. "You will see God help you through this. It will get easier. I promise you will make it. And someday, you'll be the one offering comfort to another, like I'm doing now. I get to share the hope I have with you. You'll see. God won't waste this pain."

God sent us just the people we needed to help us keep moving forward. I needed help with even the most basic things in life, like eating and drinking. That same day, some friends who were sitting with me encouraged me to take a few sips of water and eat a few bites of food. Something so mundane had suddenly become an enormous task. I was able to eat a few bites, but just barely. Food repulsed me, and my body felt like it wanted to shut down.

When I woke on the third morning, June 9, my mom greeted me with a huge hug. I could tell by the look on her face that she had something important to share with me.

"Anne, you won't believe what happened this morning," she said. "Just wait until I tell you what God did for me!"

With tears in her eyes, she related to me an encounter she'd had with the Lord. Early that morning, while it was still dark, she had left her bed and gone to the kitchen. Sleep had eluded her, so she sought the Lord instead. She sat in the dimly lit kitchen and asked God, "How do I do this? How do I give thanks in *this*?"

"Anne," she told me, "giving thanks felt utterly impossible. When I opened my Bible to a random page, it fell to the book of Psalms. My eyes landed on David's praises to God. Those were the exact words I needed." She told me how reading the Psalms felt like God was feeding her the thing her heart needed most—Himself.

"I asked God for help to do the impossible." She paused. "Then I thanked Him for the years He gave me with Jacob as my son here on earth. I wept with the Lord and surrendered all my pain to Him."

She had unintentionally been avoiding Him, she explained. She had been trying to survive this in her own strength. But only through total surrender and releasing her pain to God did her soul have room to receive His tender mercies and strength.

"God did something in me this morning," Mom said. "Anne,

after I surrendered to Him, I was instantly hungry for food, and I felt stronger than I have since this all began. I know we will survive this. For the first time, I truly know I will survive. And I have to tell anyone who is suffering—the only way to make it through is to surrender to the Father and trust Him to carry you."

Just two days after God had gently turned my face toward His, He met my mom in her deep need and led her to Himself in a moment of full, childlike surrender. The same would happen for Daddy and Liz, though not through such distinct encounters. They also turned to Jesus, but for them it didn't happen all at once. And that's okay. There is no timeline for grief, nor is there a rulebook for suffering. For each of us, turning to God with our broken hearts was our salvation—a gift from Him. Scripture says we can't even choose Jesus without His help to do it. We have nothing. He is everything.

Whether in one significant moment or little by little, what matters is that we all turned our faces to our Great Healer. A beloved hymn from childhood took on deeper meaning in those days. As the hymn says:

> Turn your eyes upon Jesus.
> Look full in His wonderful face.
> And the things of earth will grow strangely dim,
> In the light of His glory and grace.

I'm thankful God met my mom that morning because she would desperately need His strength for the days ahead, when she would be planning and attending her baby's funeral.

Preparing for Goodbye

We wanted Jacob's funeral to honor him—to glorify God and be full of all the things Jacob loved. Most of the decisions were obvious—a rustic wooden casket and flower arrangements filled with duck decoys, hay, and cattails. The service would include music, memories of Jacob, and the reading of God's Word.

My sweet mama had her heart set on someone who loved Jacob singing at his memorial. As she asked each potential singer in our family, they all declined. They knew how difficult it would be to make it through a song at Jacob's funeral without completely breaking down. When my parents had exhausted their options, Mom was heartbroken to think there would be no special song to honor Jacob.

On Friday afternoon, my parents sat together in the dining room, and Mom spoke again about how much she wished someone would sing a hymn or worship song at the memorial. She couldn't stop crying.

"What are we going to do?" she asked.

"Honey," my dad said, "why does this song matter so much to you?"

"This will be our last chance to honor Jacob, to show how loved he was," she said. "And . . . I want to praise Jesus. I want everyone to know how much we still love Jesus, even now."

"Then let's pray about it," Daddy said. He took her hands in his, and they bowed their heads. Daddy prayed that God would provide someone to sing to honor Jacob and that their song would glorify Jesus' name. He prayed that if this weren't God's will, He would remove my mom's desire for it and put her heart at ease. "Whatever You decide, God, we'll be okay with," he concluded. "Let Your will be done. Amen."

With that, my parents left the matter in God's hands. Daddy stood from the table and went outside to water the flowers he and Jacob had recently planted. Before Jacob died, he and Daddy had been in the middle of a landscaping renovation they had been doing themselves to save money. For months, Daddy did his best to keep those flowers alive. In the aftermath of Jacob's death, those flowers held great importance.

As Daddy went outside, I came downstairs completely unaware of my parents' conversation and prayer and headed straight for the piano. This was the first time since the early hours of June 7 that no one outside of our little family was in our house, and I wanted to spend that time worshiping God. I had been playing the piano every day since Jacob died, which I often did even before losing him; but this day, with just our family home, I felt the need to offer something more. So I sang the words of a song out loud to God.

The melody and words of "What a Beautiful Name" floated through the house and into my soul. As I worshiped, I began to feel a hint of joy for the first time since Jacob died. I sang about the power of Jesus' name and felt peace wash over me and settle in my heart. I could finally breathe freely. Since the night I'd learned the news, every breath had felt like a struggle. But praising the name of my Jesus brought relief to my hurting heart.

Lost in the comfort I was feeling in the Lord's presence, I didn't hear my mom walk into the room. I didn't realize anyone was listening until she spoke.

"Anne, I had no idea you could sing." My mom stood quietly crying in the doorway.

"I don't sing," I said matter-of-factly. I lifted my fingers off the keys and turned toward my mom. "I'm just worshiping God right now."

She took a deep breath. "Honey," she began, "we can't find anyone to sing at your brother's funeral." She paused. "Do you think you could do it?"

At first, I felt resistant to her request and even a little angry. "Of course I can't do that, Mom," I said. "There's no way." But as soon as the words left my mouth, I questioned them. I knew I should talk to God. So I told Mom I would pray about it.

I walked into my bedroom and shut the door. I sat on my bed, bowing my head. "God, if You want me to sing at Jacob's funeral, You have to tell me that's what You want."

And in that still, quiet moment, He did. Ever since I invited Jesus into my life, the main way I've understood His will is through a feeling of peace. In that moment, as I sought His direction, I felt the familiar peace of the Lord's leading wash over me. I knew exactly what it meant. God wanted me to sing at Jacob's funeral.

"Mom," I said, walking down the stairs. "I asked God, and He wants me to sing at Jacob's funeral. So I will."

I was now at peace with the decision, so the Enemy turned his attack on my mom. She later told me that as soon as I'd agreed to sing at the funeral, fears suddenly bombarded her mind. Would I fail and feel embarrassed in front of everyone? For a split second she questioned the decision. But as quickly as the thoughts came, she captured and silenced them. She decided it didn't matter if I messed up. We were doing this for God's glory, not our own. The decision was made. I would sing at Jacob's funeral.

"Oh, Anne." Mom grabbed me and pulled me into her arms. "Thank you so much."

"You're welcome, Mom," I said, returning her hug in full. I pulled back and looked her in the eye. "I know God said to do it, so I will. But it is a little intimidating—I've never sung in front of anyone before . . . but I know this isn't about me. This is about glorifying Jesus and honoring Jacob. I'd risk anything for that."

I chose to sing "What a Beautiful Name," the very song my mother had overheard me singing. I called two friends and asked them to accompany me. Carson, a girl I'd been friends with since I was little, agreed to play violin. And Hayes, who had been my classmate for many years, said yes to playing his guitar. They came over the next day to rehearse the song, and we practiced again at the church on Sunday during the funeral rehearsal. Before that rehearsal, my family decided to attend the Sunday morning church service.

When we entered the sanctuary that morning, we felt the eyes of many people turn toward us in surprise. Those who knew us couldn't believe we were out in public just five days after Jacob's death. But the Holy Spirit had drawn us there, with our weary souls and our swollen eyes. We had initially debated whether to attend, but that morning each of us felt the same pull of the Great Shepherd: "Come to Me, all who are weary and burdened, and I will give you rest" (Matthew 11:28 NASB). Though we barely felt alive, we knew we needed to be in the house of the Lord that day.

Reverend Randle saw us walk in the doors and felt the

simultaneous hush of compassion and pity from the congregation. He came directly to us and wrapped his arms around each of us. The sorrow he felt for us was evident as he led us to our seats. My parents, Liz, and I huddled together on the wooden pew as the service began and the sweet strains of familiar hymns surrounded us.

As we sang, I envisioned Jacob sitting beside me, worshiping Jesus with his rich baritone voice. I imagined him turning to smile at me, as he had done so many times before. I was surprised to feel God's presence so intensely. Through an ordinary Sunday morning service, God ministered to our weary souls. Church was the best place we could have been that day. The Lord held us close and tenderly poured His love into our broken hearts—knowing that the very next day we would walk out those same doors with Jacob's casket.

A Note from Anne

If you are wounded or hurting today, the best advice I can give you is this: turn your heart toward God. Whatever you are feeling, He can handle it—all of it. The tears, screams, questions, or silent thoughts—He invites you to share all of it with Him and let Him tend to your heart. God is not scared of your emotions. He is a tender Shepherd.

My mother, father, sister, and I each turned to God in different ways and at different times. I strongly believe that submitting our heartache to Him was the only reason we made it through the loss of Jacob. We couldn't do it on our own, though we sometimes tried. But every time we turned to God with our pain, we found comfort and relief. It didn't suddenly make everything all better or take away our feelings of loss. Not at all. But as we brought our broken hearts and overwhelming emotions to God, we received strength to keep going and peace amid the pain.

Worship was the primary way I turned my heart toward God. Many times, worship meant sitting at the piano and singing. Other times it looked like putting on a worship song, lying on my bed, and just breathing. Sometimes all I could do was listen as my Bible app read aloud verses from the Bible. That, too, is worship, because worship is a posture of your heart—a turning toward God—and acknowledging who He really is. Whatever you are going through, I encourage you to bring your hurting heart to Jesus. He will give you rest.

> "Come to me, all of you who are weary and carry heavy burdens, and I will give you rest."
>
> Matthew 11:28 NLT

FIVE

Offering My Song

THE DAY OF MY BROTHER'S FUNERAL DAWNED CLEAR AND beautiful, the welcome sun shining down on our weary souls. Rising from my mattress on my parents' floor, I walked on autopilot to the upstairs bathroom. I mindlessly brushed my teeth and washed my face. Then I walked to my bedroom to get dressed. This morning, the nightmare we'd been waking to each morning held a new sorrow—we would begin to say our final goodbyes to Jacob.

I pulled on my black dress, sliding my arms into its ruffled sleeves. Any other day, I'd have been thrilled to wear the pretty outfit. But that day, I would have rather been wearing anything else but a black funeral dress. I stared at my reflection in the mirror, seeing sorrow etched in every contour of my face. My brain struggled to grasp reality. *This can't be happening,* my mind screamed. *There is no way I'm actually getting dressed for Jacob's funeral right now. This cannot be real!*

But it was real. The anxious, sinking feeling deep inside reminded me that this was not a dream. As much as I hated the fact, I was preparing to say goodbye to my brother for good.

I stood transfixed as my mind drifted to a day five years earlier, when I had said a different kind of goodbye to Jacob. He was about to leave for his freshman year of college at the Citadel, which was eight hours from home. The day before he left, our family went out for dinner together. I was dreading Jacob's departure to an out-of-state school because it meant I would not see him again until Christmas. I couldn't imagine going four months without my big brother. I was ten, he was eighteen; and in my eyes, he was a hero.

Jacob knew how hard his leaving was going to be on me, and he pulled me aside for a private goodbye that night. When dinner was over, Jacob motioned for me to follow him outside. He draped his arm around my shoulders and smiled down at me. Reaching into his pocket, he pulled out a five-dollar bill.

"Here you go, Annie," he said. "This is for you. I want you to use it to buy a milkshake and cheer yourself up tomorrow. Don't worry, the time will fly by."

I took the bill and sniffled. "Thank you, Jacob," I said. "But I don't want a milkshake. I just want you to stay. Do you really have to leave?"

"Yes, I do, little Annie," he said, "but I promise it'll be okay. Before you know it, we'll be back on the farm together like no time at all has passed."

I gave a weak smile and tucked the money into my pocket. I tried to believe him, but four months felt like a very long time to a fifth grader. I gave my big brother a tight squeeze and whispered, "I love you, Jacob."

"I love you too, Annie."

I never bought a milkshake with that five-dollar bill. In fact, I took it home and put it in a special box Jacob had carved for me a few years earlier. And to this day, that five dollars is in my bedroom, where I can look at it and remember Jacob's tender goodbye and his attempt to cheer me up that night.

Now here I was, fifteen and about to say a much longer and more definite goodbye to my brother. Once again, I tried to believe that it would feel like no time at all before I would be with Jacob. But a lifetime seems like a very long time.

"Anne, it's almost time to go." My dad's voice pulled me out of my reverie. Slowly I turned from the mirror to finish preparing. My family and I readied ourselves the best we could and left in the early afternoon to go to the church together. It was a quiet ride. Daddy drove in total silence, staring straight ahead the whole time. The quiet was punctuated only by Mom's occasional sniffles. Liz was crying too. I simply leaned my head against the window. Words seemed inadequate for the heaviness of the moment.

Honoring Jacob

There would be two funeral services for Jacob, both exactly the same, led by Reverend Randle. The first was held on Monday, June 12, at Tates Creek Presbyterian Church in Lexington. The second would take place on Tuesday, June 13, at the Wilson family church in the town near our farm. And there, on the family farm, we would lay my brother to rest.

I felt a nervous churning inside as a new level of anxiety filled me that Monday. In a few short hours, I would play and sing in front of others for the first time ever, and we were expecting more than a thousand people to come and honor Jacob. As we neared the church, my fear increased. I worried that I would have an emotional breakdown mid-song or that I would make too many mistakes and ruin my tribute to Jacob. I also worried that the pain we all were facing that day would be too much for us to bear.

"God, I need You," I whispered as we pulled into the church parking lot. "You said to do this, so I'm counting on *You* to get me through. I know I can't make it through on my own."

Before the funeral began, we held a visitation for Jacob at the church so anyone who wanted could personally greet us. Friends and family and even people we didn't know came to say goodbye to Jacob. Some came whom we hadn't seen in many years. Everyone arrived with tears, hugs, and stories about Jacob. The incredible stories I heard about my brother that day were each a little balm to my soul. I loved hearing how much he meant to others. Each story also brought a flood of memories of the brother I had just lost. It ached all the way to my bones, and my tears never stopped flowing.

The constant stream of visitors began to taper as we neared the start of the service. Each pew filled, and friends and family took their seats in the reverent hush. Before long, there was no more room to sit. My heart swelled with gratitude as I gazed over the crowd. I wished Jacob were there to see all these loved ones who had come to honor him.

Each member of our immediate family chose to honor Jacob that day in their own way. Elizabeth played a beautiful rendition of "In Christ Alone" on the piano. But halfway through her performance, the pain of it all quickly overwhelmed her, and she could not finish. I feel certain the hearts of everyone in that place went out to her when she eventually gave up and fled the stage in tears.

The reverend called us to worship, and we stood to sing "It Is Well with My Soul." I had often heard the story of this familiar old hymn written by Horatio G. Spafford. He wrote it as a tribute to God's goodness amid unfathomable suffering. Just after losing all four of his precious daughters at sea, he penned the words, "Whatever my lot, Thou hast taught me to say, it is well, it is well with my soul." Our family joined in singing the beautiful hymn because, despite our great sorrow in losing Jacob, we desired to declare God's goodness and love.

After further Scripture readings and songs, the time came for my parents to deliver their tributes to Jacob. They knew they could not stand and read what they had written, so they asked loved ones to stand for them to read their parting words for their son.

My mother wrote a devastatingly beautiful letter to Jacob, which Aunt Nene stood to read in her stead. Aunt Nene struggled to get through the words as she shared this tribute for Jacob:

Dear Jacob,

From the first moment I held you in my arms, it seems you peered into my soul and created a new space in my heart. I had never experienced a love like this. The world became a more beautiful place . . . full of wonder and anticipation . . . ready for your enthusiasm and boundless energy and influence. From your youngest years, you were full of questions, insight, and adventures. From being Batman, Superman, to a ransom ole cowboy, this kept life so busy for me. Then we started to see this little boy seek new adventures and discoveries. Your dad and I were surprised when you wanted to lose your training wheels at the age of three. And not many second graders could boast of helping their dad install hardwood floors, but then again, you were never a boaster . . . but rather a young man of action. Baseball became your "full-time job" in the elementary years, and you had the once-in-a-lifetime opportunity to be part of a team that won the Little League state tournament. From one adventure to the next, I had to be ready at all times to take your hand and follow. You were such a *leader* and helped me experience a life of fun times.

I planned to shape and grow you into a young man who would impact the world, but it was *you* who grew *me* in so many ways. I am a teacher at heart, and yet you had many lessons for me. You showed me that patience can always grow a deeper reservoir and that choosing a different path can lead to blessing and honor. You walked to the beat of your own drum and inspired me to realize that all children should get that opportunity. We would always say, "Jacob, you always take the road less traveled."

It seems this world could not quite contain your larger-than-life approach. And so with an ocean of tears, we must say goodbye to you for a season. And to my sweet precious son, Jacob, I want you to know that you made us all *so very proud* during your time on this side of eternity. You once told me that you had so much fun as a child you wished you could *rewind the tape*. It is me now who wishes I could rewind and do it all again. Being your mother was one of the greatest honors of my life, and with every breath I continue to take, I will cherish that memory and carry you forward in my heart always. I bet you have talked nonstop since you arrived on Wednesday. Convince Jesus to start a Ducks Unlimited Chapter in heaven! I can see you hunting and fishing at this very moment. Knowing that you are in paradise with Jesus is the only thing that gives me comfort and allows my heart to go on.

Forever love to my dear
precious son, Jacob,
Mom

My father also wrote a moving tribute to Jacob. His was in the form of a heart-wrenching poem. He asked our Uncle Steve to read it aloud that day. Uncle Steve's tears flowed as he read my father's words for Jacob:

He was gently placed into his mother's arms;
She held him closely and protected him
from harm.
He took his first step and was excited and
proud;
His joy could not be contained as he laughed
out loud.
A fireman, a superhero, or maybe a cowboy
today;
He was so cute as we watched him play.
He was so excited for his first day at school
at last;
He gave his mom a hug and ran into class.
We overflowed with joy when we heard
him say,
"I asked Jesus to come into my heart today!"
He walked off the stage with his diploma
in hand;
No longer a boy but becoming a man.
The last of his things were carried into
his room;
How could he be going to college so soon?
He had his degree and began his future plan;
No longer a boy, he had become a man.
My little boy grew up, I was so proud of him;
He had become my very best friend.
His future was bright, he was ready to soar;
He was ready to live like never before.

But God had another plan for his life;
He did not want him to experience this world's
strife.
It was time to leave this world, no longer
to roam;
Well done, my faithful servant, it is time to
come home.

Love,
Dad

When Uncle Steve was finished reading, it was my turn. I stood from my seat on the front pew and began to walk to the piano onstage. I took one slow step after another up the red-carpeted stairs, a shaky nervousness filling my body. It was the same sensation I'd felt for days, only magnified. I reached the piano and turned to look out across the sea of faces in the crowd. Friends and family members looked back at me with tears in their eyes. Had I not been feeling such a dark sense of loss, I would have been thrilled to see so many loved ones gathered in such a majestic place. It was beautiful, but I couldn't appreciate the beauty of it. I was overwhelmed by both the ache of goodbye and seeing hundreds of people staring at me. A few friends gave me encouraging nods as I took a seat. It was time to worship my Jesus.

I took a deep breath and smoothed my dress to calm my shaking hands. I was about to sing for the first time in front of twelve hundred people. Would I even be able to make it through? Would my hands stop shaking enough to let me play?

As I gently placed my fingers on the keys, I looked up to God for a brief second, imploring Him for help. At that very moment, God removed every nervous feeling from my body. The fear and worry were gone. I looked at my fingers and saw steadiness—the shaking was gone. *Thank You, God!* With a heart suddenly at peace, I took in a deep breath and prepared to sing.

As Carson, Hayes, and I began to play the intro to the song, I heard God's voice again. His words, interjected at such a pivotal moment, would change my life completely: *Anne. This is what I'm calling you to do. I'm calling you to praise and worship My name.*

I had no doubt the voice was the Lord's. I will never forget those words.

With a confidence that could only come from God's Spirit, I began to play and sing "What a Beautiful Name," a song that magnifies the powerful, wonderful name of Jesus. The song speaks of His longing for us to join Him in heaven and tells of His victory over death and the grave. The song was a cool drink of water to my parched soul, and I prayed it was the same for everyone who heard it that day.

That day, I sang for Jacob, and I sang to worship my Jesus. Without tears, without stopping, and without breaking down, I offered my song for them both. The ability to sing such powerful words at such a sorrowful time without breaking down was only possible through God's strength and His Spirit. Now, more than ever, my family and I wanted to praise the name of Jesus. We all realized in a terrible and wonderful way how short life really is and how it can change in an instant. We longed to tell the world of the hope found in Jesus' beautiful name. I knew that was what Jacob would want too.

I lifted my fingers from the keys as the final notes of my song rang throughout the sanctuary. I exhaled a deep sigh of relief. The faces I had just feared were smiling at me through tears. Many held tissues to their eyes.

As I returned to my seat, God impressed another thing on my heart: I would never be an astronaut. *I have called you to a life of worship through music,* He said. I could never have imagined that God would speak to me about my future at such a moment, and even less that He would call me to a life of music. But somehow, I just believed Him. In that moment, I had no doubt the Lord would fulfill this calling on my life. I knew that meant I wasn't going to be an astronaut, and I was okay with that knowledge. In the aftermath of losing Jacob, the dream of being an astronaut didn't seem important anymore. With Jacob in heaven and a huge hole in my heart, I barely had a will to live, much less to pursue the dream of going to space. I did not feel even an ounce of grief at the thought of leaving that childhood dream behind. I actually felt peace. The desire to go to space was simply gone.

Losing Jacob changed everything, including my dreams for my life. I now knew I would have a future in music, worshiping and praising the name of Jesus. God must have given me a gift of faith to accept such a sudden change in direction and believe that He would fulfill that calling. I had no idea how or when His new plan for me would happen or what that calling would entail.

I just knew it would *be*. Someday. Because God said so, and I believed Him.

A Message of New Life

Those who attended the funeral that day later told me about two things that stood out to them from the service. The first was my ability to make it through my song. The second was the invocation Pastor Cameron gave and his presentation of the gospel. The most important thing to our family was that the good news of Jesus Christ be shared at Jacob's funeral. What better way to honor him than to offer true life to all who came to say goodbye? So prior to Scripture reading and Reverend Randle's message of comfort and hope, we asked Pastor Cameron to present the gospel.

As he spoke, he shared a story about his sister and her husband from years before. Ashley and Matt had once offered Cameron and his wife, Erica, a trip to join them at an all-inclusive resort in Cancun. All Cameron and Erica had to do was purchase their plane tickets.

"Deal!" Pastor Cameron said, recalling the moment. "We looked forward to this trip for weeks—we planned, we packed, we talked about the white sandy beaches. This trip would be amazing!"

But when they arrived at the airport on the day they were supposed to fly off to a tropical paradise together, Cameron and Erica found out they couldn't go. They didn't have their six-month-old son's birth certificate. He was their firstborn, and they had not received his birth certificate yet. Having never flown overseas with a baby before, they didn't realize they needed it for the flight.

"We had to stand at the window and watch Matt and Ashley fly off without us," Pastor Cameron said. "We were incredibly sad. Fortunately, we were able to expedite the birth certificate and join them in paradise a few days later."

When Pastor Cameron finished this story, he talked about losing Matt a few years earlier. It was the same story he'd shared with our class the first day I'd met him. Paster Cameron said that at his brother-in-law's funeral, the officiant told the story about the airport and ended with "He's done it again. Matt has flown off to paradise and left us all behind."

Pastor Cameron paused in the emotion of the moment. "We are all at the gate right now," he said. "Jacob has flown off to paradise without us, and this is either our final goodbye or only our 'see you later.' Asking Jesus to be your Lord and Savior is the only way to be saved from sin and death. It's the only way to see Jacob again in heaven one day."

He ended with these words: "The devil will never tell you there is no hell, and he will never tell you there is no heaven. He will only tell you that there is no hurry. But the Word of God says, 'Today is the day of salvation.' Today if you hear the voice of the Lord, do not harden your heart."

Many people heard God's voice calling to them that day. Heaven rejoiced—and I believe Jacob rejoiced—as lives were forever changed and new names were added to the Book of Life. That was the sweetest gift we could have received from God—seeing new life spring up so soon following Jacob's death.

Final Farewell

The next day, we held the exact same service at the family church in the town near the farm. The second service was just as meaningful, and painful, as the first. After the service, we drove to the Wilson Family Farm, Jacob's favorite place on earth, and we laid my brother to rest. Only our closest friends and family joined us at the farm for Jacob's burial service. An intimate graveside setting had been created just for Jacob. After Pastor Cameron shared a parting word with us, Jacob's friends stood and solemnly honored him with a final duck call.

That's when I broke. As the sounds of the final duck call echoed across the hills, my strength gave out and the grief hit me at a level I had not yet experienced. The rest of my family had already had these moments, but I had not. God had been holding me up and speaking through me to comfort my family. But now it was my turn to fall apart and fall into His arms.

I fell to the ground and wrapped my arms around my brother's casket, weeping to the point of screaming. "Jacob! Jacob, *no*, Jacob! Please, Jacob!"

I kept calling his name. I would not—*could not*—let go. This final goodbye was more than my soul could bear. My mother tried to calm me, but I could not be comforted. I could not let go. It felt as though my soul were fracturing with the effort of saying goodbye.

Pastor Cameron knelt beside me and put his arm around my shoulders, offering support as long as I needed it. Eventually, I calmed enough to hear my family say, "It's time, Anne. It's time to go." My strength was spent. I stood shakily and turned to walk away. I cannot adequately describe the sadness of that duck call or the despair I felt turning to walk away from Jacob's grave. It was a grief too deep for words.

As I slowly headed toward Granddaddy's house for a small reception, I turned to look back one last time. There was Sallie, Jacob's hunting dog, sitting next to his grave. She refused to leave, just as I had. Poor, sweet Sallie sat there for nearly an hour with sad brown eyes fixed on her master's grave. Jacob was her person, and she, too, was facing the reality that he was gone.

In the weeks that followed, Sallie would sometimes hide from us and cry the most mournful sounds you can imagine. Her cries kept us up at night. We took her to the vet, hoping to find a way to help Jacob's sweet dog. The vet told us Sallie was grieving Jacob and we had to allow her to go through the process of mourning him, just as we all were doing. The sad cries did finally subside, but Sallie was never the same. Her health began to go downhill after that, and we lost her four years after losing Jacob. She's now buried out on the farm.

The days of Jacob's funerals and burial are tender places in my heart and memories. Those memories are painful to recall, yet I often do. I think back on offering my song for Jacob and the Lord. I think about how I heard God's voice that day and received His call on my life. It's not at all what I had planned. A music career was nothing I ever expected or even wanted. Like I told my mom when she first asked me to perform at the funeral, "I don't sing." But in my heart, I knew God would complete whatever He had begun to do in my life. Like the Bible says, the One who called me would be faithful to bring it to completion, and I could leave it in His hands (Philippians 1:6).

I didn't tell a soul about the words God spoke to me that day, not even my mom. I kept those precious words to myself for more than a year. At first, I kept it quiet because I wasn't ready to admit that my carefully laid plans of becoming an astronaut had completely changed. I had been so intent on them for the past three years, I didn't know what others would think about the new plan God had given me. The truth was, everything had changed, including the trajectory of my life. I didn't know where I was headed, but I knew the One who would get me there.

A Note from Anne

None of us knows what the next day may bring. I never suspected I would lose my precious brother on that June morning. When it happened, it nearly destroyed me. Nearly, but it didn't. Because God was there, speaking life to me and tenderly caring for me through the pain. Out of Jacob's death, God gave me a destiny! Only He could do that. From the earliest moments of unspeakable grief, He was there, bringing about good in my life.

When your pain and sorrow go deep, God's love goes deeper. He will meet you there. He will also work it for your good. That can be a tough truth to swallow. I know. But goodness is part of His nature, and He wants you to know and experience it. This is the difficult reality: We can only fully understand how God brings life out of death and joy out of mourning when we have walked through it. If you are struggling right now, pray this prayer with me: "God, don't waste an ounce of this pain. Work all of this for my good and Your glory."

> We know that God causes all things to work together for good to those who love God, to those who are called according to His purpose.
>
> Romans 8:28 NASB

SIX

Through the Valley

TEN DAYS AFTER LOSING JACOB, I RETURNED TO THE Wilson Farm for the first time since his burial. My family and I needed to feel close to Jacob, and the farm provided that for us. Every step I took there was thick with memory. The familiar rolling hills stretched out before me as I trekked through the pine trees and walked by the barn filled with the earthy aroma of the horses. Everywhere I looked, every sound I heard, every smell I inhaled—it all reminded me of being there with Jacob.

As my family gathered inside Granddaddy's house for lunch, I slipped away for some time alone. I knew exactly where I was headed. A hill about half a mile from the farmhouse had always been one of my favorite places to go with Jacob. On that hill Jacob taught me to handle, load, and shoot a gun. We had spent many happy hours up there shooting together.

The weekend before his accident, Jacob and I had stood on that very hill for some target practice. Now I made the climb to the top without him by my side. As I walked the well-worn path, I heard only the rustle of my own footsteps and the lonely call of the turtledove from a nearby tree. When I reached the top, my gaze fell upon shotgun shells scattered around our makeshift shooting range. My breath caught in my throat and tears threatened to spill over as I realized those shells were the very ones that fell as Jacob and I shot together the weekend before his accident.

"All right, Annie," Jacob had said, looking at me intently. "Show me. Loaded correctly? Safety on? Okay. Bring it up and aim. Let's see what you've got." I released the safety, took a deep breath, and exhaled as I fired, just like he had taught me to do. The sound of my shot echoed through the hills.

"Ha! Look at that shot, Jacob!" I laughed. "Dead on the target."

"Not bad, not bad," Jacob said as I re-engaged the safety and handed the gun back to him, beaming. "You make me proud, little Annie."

Standing on that same hill a few weeks later, I almost lost myself in the tempting thought that nothing had changed and Jacob and I would be here shooting again soon. Our shells were right there. Surely, we'd be adding to them in a little while, and he'd give me another lesson. I still had so much to learn from him. But just a turn of my head brought reality into clear focus as my eyes fell upon Granddaddy's barn and Jacob's grave.

I can't face it right now, I thought, averting my eyes. Even so, I reluctantly began the descent and headed toward the gravesite. Whether I was ready or not, I was drawn to it.

As I approached, I tested my heart with each tentative step

to see if it could handle this. My breaths became shallow and my heart pounded, thinking of that piece of earth and what it held. At home, I had been distracting myself from the pain and the reality of losing Jacob. I was terrified of accepting that he was really gone, fearing that the full force of it would destroy me. Instead, I pushed down the truth and busied myself with other things.

As I neared the grave, instead of feeling despair as I expected, peace welled up inside. I sat down on the soft earth, and there, in the exact spot where I'd broken under the weight of my deepest pain, God comforted me. He allowed me to stare my brother's death in the face and see that it would not destroy me. Death did not have the final word after all. Instead of the anguish I expected, Jacob's grave produced a precious and beautiful ache inside me.

Over the next weeks and months, I was drawn back many times to sit by Jacob's grave. As I sat there, I often read the Word of God, reminding myself of the greatest truth—that Jesus defeated sin and death once and for all. I love the words of 1 Corinthians 15:55 and 57, which say, "O death, where is your sting? O grave, where is your victory? . . . But thanks be to God, who gives us the victory through our Lord Jesus Christ!" (MEV). I knew Jacob was experiencing the ultimate victory, and God was offering me victory too—victory over my hopelessness and my fear. Each time I sat at Jacob's grave, I realized anew that he was not in that grave any more than Jesus was still in the tomb. That knowledge helped me face the loss of my brother with hope—at least when I was on the farm. Every other day, I still did my best to distract myself from the awful truth that he was gone.

Struggling to Cope

July went by in a blur as we adjusted to life without Jacob. Surviving till the end of each day felt like a major accomplishment. We walked through those dark days all carrying a similar wound, but we did not all face it the same way. My dad grieved in private, doing his best to stay strong for his family. He didn't like to talk about what happened, lest he show the world his deeply broken heart, so he kept it mostly to himself. Liz, too, was closed off and reserved with her pain. She spoke of our tragedy only to her close inner circle. And although my mom struggled to speak of Jacob at first, she eventually found healing in telling stories about him and revealing to others the deep pain she was experiencing.

I longed to talk about Jacob. When I did, it almost felt like he was still with us. I needed to remember every detail of our times together and could not bear the thought of forgetting them—that would dishonor my brother. Sometimes it was hard for those around me to know how to respond when I talked about Jacob. My friends would try to cheer me up by changing the subject. I knew their intentions were kind, but deep down I didn't want the subject to change. Jacob was too important. There was no cheering me up.

From that very first excruciating night without my brother, I had been trying to be strong for those around me, especially my hurting family. During the first few days, God had given me supernatural strength and wisdom to share with them. As the days went by, I tried to be the strong one in my own power. I didn't want to add to anyone's grief by openly displaying mine, so I hid my internal struggle. Losing Jacob was my first real experience with grief and the first time I felt completely powerless. I didn't know how to cope. I thought hiding my grief was what was best for all of us, but it wasn't best for me. This only kept me stuck in the denial of what had happened. If you don't accept there is something to grieve, you cannot fully move through it. And that is what I was doing, even though I didn't know it at the time.

During those first few months, every time we heard Jacob's voice in an old voice mail or watched him in a video, it triggered an emotional breakdown. To this day, I feel physically ill when I watch a video of Jacob. But my mom's reaction was the most painful to see.

One day, just a month after Jacob left us, Mom came across a video of Jacob on her phone. As she saw his smile and heard his familiar voice, she cried out in what sounded like a muffled scream. The intensity of her grief scared me, and rather than add to her pain by showing mine, I held in my tears and went to hold my mom. I wrapped my arms around her as she wept.

"Mom, Jacob isn't in pain anymore," I said softly. "He's not suffering. He's in heaven with Jesus right now."

As I said those words, the sobs wracking her body began to subside and she took a deep, shuddering breath. Every time Liz or I reminded her that Jacob was in paradise with Jesus, the truth seemed to bring her a measure of peace. Instead of joining in her grief, I pushed mine down, hoping my support would give her some relief. I did this with my whole family, but especially with my mom. I didn't want to make her pain worse, and I thought showing her mine would do that. So in my attempt to protect my parents and sister from further hurt, I repressed my own pain most of the time.

As a fifteen-year-old, it's scary seeing your parents—the strong ones in your life—walk through such horrific grief. They experienced such deep pain that at times I feared it would destroy them. Literally. I used to sneak into their bedroom at night just to make sure they were still alive and hadn't died in their sleep. I feared that the grief might be too much and their bodies would just give out from it. I tried to do all I could to ease their pain. They never asked me to do any of this; I took it on myself. Had they known my struggle, I know they would have done anything in their power to help me.

"I'm okay" was my normal response when people asked how I was doing. "It's hard, but I'm okay." I just kept pushing through one day after another. I said I was okay, but on the inside, I was the furthest thing from okay.

When I was grieving, people told me, "Time heals all wounds." But this didn't feel true to me at all. As weeks turned into months, healing didn't "just happen." From the outside, I appeared to be living the life of a normal teenager, but each step was exhausting. I did trust Jesus, and I ran to Him for healing, but I also locked down my emotions to avoid showing weakness. I smiled when I wanted to cry, portraying a strength I didn't feel. I don't think I realized what I was doing. At the time, I was doing what I thought I needed to do to survive, but my outer person and my inner person were deeply out of sync. Eventually, that would catch up with me.

The Secret Place

At the end of each day, I would crawl into my bed to be alone with God. It was a place of safety for me. I was reminded of the words of Psalm 27:5, which say, "For in the day of trouble he will keep me safe in his dwelling; he will hide me in the shelter of his sacred tent and set me high upon a rock" (NIV). In this intimate space, I would finally let some of my tears out. I cried with the Lord and wrote my pent-up feelings in my journal—words too difficult to speak out loud. No matter what I processed or asked of God, I always concluded every journal entry the same way: "God got me through another day."

As time passed, I had an increasing number of questions for God. While I did not go the route of anger in my grief, I did go the route of asking, "Why?" *Why Jacob? Why so young? Why in the prime of his life? Why my brother? Why when we all still needed him?*

These questions plagued me, and I wrestled with why any of this had happened the way it did. The constant pain made me desperate for answers, as if the answers would somehow make it all okay or relieve the deep ache I felt. *If I can just understand* why *this happened,* I thought, *then maybe I can accept it.* But what I really needed was Jesus' presence and comfort. I needed those things way more than I needed understanding. I see that now, but at the time, all I wanted was answers.

Sometimes the hopelessness and pain were so heavy that I begged God to take me home to heaven. I asked Him to just go ahead and rescue all four of us out of this earthly life so our family could be whole again and the pain would be over. And one day, He had a response for me.

That night I lay in my bed praying. *God, I can't do this anymore,* I told Him. *The pain is too much for me. I just want to be with You and with Jacob.* Tears coursed down my face, and I curled up in a ball, drenching my pillowcase. *Take all of us home to You together,* I begged. *That's what I want the most, God,* please. *Please just take me home.*

Your time is not yet finished on this earth. I instantly recognized the kind, strong voice of my Father, and I stilled. This was the voice I knew and loved—the voice I heard so clearly the night Jacob died and the voice that called me to trust Him and worship Him through music. When I heard that voice and those words, I knew I must stay in this life because God still had a plan for me. I had not yet accomplished what He had created me to do.

As His words sank into my mind and heart, I unclenched my body. My breathing slowed. He had heard my cry and answered me with gentle yet decided words that pierced through the pain. Even in my brokenness, I knew God had a good plan for my life.

As I lay there contemplating God's response to my cry to be done here on earth, I realized something else. If Jacob were already home in heaven, he must have completed his assignments here in this life. Though that realization did not make me happy, it did make sense to me. This was not the answer I was hoping to hear (would any answer suffice?), but it did calm my anxious asking. I could choose to trust God with all our lives—mine and each member of my family—because our times were in *His* hands (Psalm 31:15). I would have to choose that kind of trust over and over again in the coming months. It took time for the *choosing* to migrate from my head down to my heart.

Other than sitting at his grave, the most comforting times I experienced in the months following Jacob's death were when I worshiped God at the piano. Many days I felt a heavy weight on my chest and shoulders. When the heaviness increased to the point where I could no longer ignore the grief, I went to the piano to worship. I would take my seat on the well-worn bench—at the piano where Jacob had once played so beautifully—and miss my brother with my whole being. I knew this was a place where I would find anesthetic for the pain. When my family heard me begin to play, they usually retreated to their bedrooms to give me time alone with God. They knew how much I needed it, and I think they could see how much it helped me.

I chose songs that declared the truth of who God is—a good Father, a Comforter, a Protector. I desperately needed to be reminded of these truths. Day after day, I sat at the piano, staring out the window to my left. When I was young, I never enjoyed the piano lessons Mom made all the Wilson children take, but after accepting Jesus in seventh grade, I began learning to play worship songs. Now I was grateful for those lessons because I could pour my heart out to God as I played those beautiful songs. And as I did, I received healing from the Lord. As I lifted my voice, I allowed God to align my heart with the truth. This was my form of surrender. Through the beautiful lyrics and melodies of worship songs, I grieved Jacob. The music accessed the parts of my soul I'd been keeping under lock and key and allowed me to let out my sorrow.

At my lowest point, I gave God the costliest gift I had to offer—worship from a broken heart. When I do go home to heaven someday, I will worship my Jesus forever. He will wipe every tear from my eye (Revelation 21:4). But only here on earth can I praise Him in the middle of pain and loss. He honors and delights in worship coming from a broken heart—a heart that declares, "God, even now—even in this—You are good."

Still, what I received from Him in return was far greater than anything I had to offer. As soon as I began worshiping my Jesus, the heaviness lifted. I knew He understood. No more fast-forwarding through His suffering, like when I was a little girl watching a movie about Him. Now I zeroed in on it and welcomed the knowledge that Jesus knew my struggle and was right in the middle of it with me. In those precious moments at the piano, I had an inner knowledge that God was going to bring something amazingly good out of Jacob's death. I didn't know what or when or how, but I knew He would redeem the pain.

A Job Season

During the first months after Jacob's death, I often feared I would end up like Job in the Bible and lose everything. I had never been prone to anxiety before, but now I experienced rising terror if my parents didn't arrive home on time. I feared that they, too, had been killed in a car accident. I often asked God, *What if my whole family dies and I become like Job and am utterly alone? If that happens, will I have the strength to still trust Your goodness, like Job did?*

We did not lose everything, but we did enter a time during which it felt that everything that could go wrong, did. Though our experience as a family was not nearly as devastating as Job's, it seemed as though we were going through a "Job season."

Shortly after losing Jacob, a pipe burst in our upstairs bathroom and flooded the house so badly that part of the first-floor ceiling caved in. While repairs were in progress, we had to move out and live in a hotel for six weeks. During that time, Mom and I had to prepare for school to start, which was always stressful, but that year it was worse because our growing school was moving to a different location. Mom's plate was full with the many tasks of preparing for the start of school right after Labor Day.

In early September we were able to move home, and we believed the worst was over. It wasn't. That fall, my dad was laid off from his job as an engineer, my mom developed shingles, and I broke my arm falling out of my bed. The break was so bad I needed surgery to repair it. None of these problems came close to the severity and heartbreak of losing Jacob. But because we were so broken emotionally, each trial felt like another heavy brick piled onto our weary backs. Our emotional reserves were drained, and we just kept getting hit with a new form of trouble. I did the best I could to put everything back into God's hands and cling to Him, even if more hardship came. But under the surface, I worried my strength would give out if just one more thing went wrong.

The Gift of Remembering

One day, my English teacher assigned our class a narrative essay. She asked us to describe a favorite memory. As I contemplated the assignment that night, the only childhood memories that came to mind involved Jacob. I thought of so many stories, but I couldn't decide which to write about. How could I choose just one?

Suddenly, a memory from four months earlier flashed through my mind. I gasped. How could I have forgotten my last bike ride with Jacob? I'm guessing the trauma I'd been through had pushed the memory to the recesses of my mind. I was overjoyed the memory came back, and I knew instantly that God had lovingly restored to me the details of that day.

My last bike ride with Jacob happened just three weeks before he died. We were on family vacation and had rented a beautiful little beach house in Seaside, Florida. We spent our days playing in the waves, warmed by the sun and covered in sand. One evening, we had all just settled in after a delicious meal, content and tired from a day of riding paddleboards. Before I headed upstairs to rest, Jacob caught hold of me.

"Hey, Annie, want to go for a bike ride with me?" he said with his charming smile. "I have a special spot to show you."

"Sure!" I said, rest forgotten. I was always up for doing something fun with Jacob.

Soon we had our bikes out on the sandy street. "How long is this ride?" I asked.

"Only a mile or so," he said. "You'll be fine!" I was slightly skeptical—and knew Jacob was prone to underplay what an endeavor like this might require. But I pedaled on, happy to be with him.

"This is gonna be a blast!" he said. His enthusiasm was contagious—at least at the start. We sailed by restaurants and happy families dining together as the sun slowly began to sink. On and on we pedaled, until I was weary and a little frustrated.

"How much longer, Jacob?" I whined. "It's been over a mile already!" My brother was not deterred.

"Only a little bit left, Annie. We're almost there!" The excitement in his voice urged me forward. I bit my tongue and kept pedaling. A few minutes later we pulled up to the most beautiful beach I'd ever seen, just as the sun began to set. Gorgeous pink and yellow clouds filled the sky and reflected off the white sandy beach. The water glistened in the soft glow of the setting sun. Not another soul was around, just Jacob and me. I was breathless.

"Isn't this worth it, Annie?" Jacob whispered. We stood together in awe of God's amazing creation.

Finally, I spoke. "Jacob, it's so beautiful!" We walked down the beach together, listening to the sound of the waves and marveling at the beauty before us. Earlier that week, Jacob had scouted out this beach and timed it perfectly so we could be there together just as the sun lit the sky with its final glory.

I was overwhelmed by the moment. "Thank you so much, Jacob!" I said, turning to hug my brother. "I love you."

"You're welcome, Annie," he said. "I love you too." I was touched that my sweet brother had done all of this just for me.

As I sat on my bed four months later, the details of that ride flooded my mind and conflicting emotions filled my heart. Joy and love welled up in me as I remembered what Jacob had done for me. I was grateful that God reminded me of it. But I was also filled with the bitter ache of missing my big brother and the reality that we would never share moments like that again in this life. I pressed my face into my pillow and wept.

Final Word

"Kent, girls, come in here! Look what I found!" My mom's voice floated down from Jacob's room on a cool October day. She had gone into his room in hopes of feeling closer to him. It was something we all did in those early days of grief.

As the three of us walked into the room, Mom sat at Jacob's desk; index cards were strewn before her. We drew near, and I immediately noticed Jacob's distinct handwriting on the cards.

"What do they say?" I asked.

"They're filled with Scripture," Mom answered, handing over a few. "Jacob wrote them." She paused, seeming puzzled. "They all have the same exact verse written on them. These were all over—in his drawers, his baskets, his desk. Just look!"

I picked up a card and examined it. As I read the words of 1 Peter 5:10 in Jacob's familiar handwriting, tears filled my eyes: "After you have suffered for a little while, the God of all grace, who called you to His eternal glory in Christ, will Himself perfect, confirm, strengthen, and establish you" (NASB).

We looked up from the cards in our hands, marveling at how often Jacob had written out the exact same scripture. Obviously, it held special significance for him, but none of us knew why. He had never spoken of it.

As I read the words again, it felt as though Jacob himself were comforting me.

From that day on, we clung to this scripture as our family verse. We laminated those precious cards, written in Jacob's hand, and each kept one for ourselves. Even after he was gone, Jacob was still giving us words to live by. When we needed strength to keep going and keep trusting, we found it in those words he had cherished. They gave us hope for tomorrow and a promise that God would not only bring us out of this suffering, but He would also use it to establish us in His greater plan.

I clung to Jacob's scripture when I needed to remember that God would yet bring something good out of the ashes of my life. In Him, I still had a destiny. I believed it because He said it, even though I often struggled to see anything beyond surviving another day.

A Note from Anne

We all experience suffering in this world, don't we? Jesus even promised it when He told us that in this life, we *will* face troubles. And yet, out of our suffering and trouble, God will establish us deeper in truth, in relationship with Him and even *in* Him—if we allow it. The promise of 1 Peter 5:10—Jacob's scripture—held true for me and holds true for you too. Suffering comes, but it doesn't have to stay forever. We can invite our God of grace into our pain and allow Him to perfect us, confirm us, strengthen us, and establish us in faith.

Maybe, like me, you have wondered why God allows suffering in our lives. One reason I have seen is that pain and suffering push us toward dependence on our Father. If He rescued us from every bit of suffering, how would this life be different from heaven where He promises to wipe away every tear? How would we grow in faith and maturity? How would we learn about the character of God? We will suffer in this life, but we can have hope. God has a purpose for us, even in our pain and sorrow. That truth helps me face another day, hour, or even minute, when I am walking through hard times. Whatever you are facing today, I pray this truth sinks deep into your heart.

> After you have suffered for a little while, the God of all grace, who called you to His eternal glory in Christ, will Himself perfect, confirm, strengthen, and establish you.
>
> 1 Peter 5:10 NASB

SEVEN

What a Beautiful Name

A MONTH AFTER JACOB'S DEATH, A DEAR TEACHER OF mine came by the house to bring us a meal. Before she left, she pulled me aside. "Anne," she said. "Would you consider making a video of the song you sang at Jacob's funeral? I would love to hear it again and worship along with you."

The thought filled me with dread. How could I relive a moment from one of the hardest days in my life?

"I don't know if I could do that," I said honestly. "I don't know how to make a video." I gave the first answer that popped into my head, and she didn't press any further.

A week later, another close family friend approached me with the same idea. "Will you make a recording of 'What a Beautiful Name,' Anne?" she asked gently. "It's something we could always have to look back on and remember Jacob."

I brushed off this request as well. August had just begun, and I was still in deep mourning. Figuring out how to make a recording of the song was the furthest thing from my mind. I didn't have the skills to do something like that. Plus, I could barely make it through each day, let alone try to make a video of that song. Yet the idea wouldn't go away. Before another month had passed, multiple friends and family members came to me individually with the exact same request. I began to wonder if it was more than coincidence.

Every time I thought about recording a video of the song, my mind filled with all the reasons I shouldn't. *You aren't good enough to sing in a video. What if people think you are doing it just to get your name out there? You're not qualified for this.* The Enemy's attack was relentless.

Around that same time, we faced our first devastating milestone—Jacob's birthday. The whole nation was anticipating this day, because his birthday fell on the same day as a rare total solar eclipse along a corridor of the United States. What they were calling the "Great American Eclipse" would take place on August 21, 2017. Many of our friends planned to make the hour-long drive to one of the locations in the "path of totality" where they could experience a total eclipse of the sun—a once-in-a-lifetime event for many. But we didn't have the emotional strength to face a joyful gathering of people. If Jacob were still with us, it would have been the most epic birthday of all. But now, the eclipse itself was overshadowed by the aching of our hearts.

Everything was opposite of what it should have been that day. Three months earlier, I would have been obsessed with this astrological event and would have certainly been following all the news on the NASA website. I would have begged my parents to take us to one of the total eclipse sites. But now it didn't matter much. We should have been celebrating Jacob's life that day, not mourning his death. Pictures of him should have filled us with pride and joy, not despair and grief.

We needed to get out of the house. So my parents, Liz, and I went to a little country cafe to have a late lunch out on the patio and watch the eclipse. The eclipse would occur from roughly 1:00 to 4:00 p.m., but I couldn't muster much enthusiasm for it. At least it was a good distraction from the longing for Jacob that threatened to overwhelm me.

We slipped on our little cardboard glasses and watched the sun slowly disappear, doing our best to maintain our composure. I couldn't help but wonder if maybe this was the day Jesus would come back to get us, and my heart leaped at the thought. But the eclipse came and went, and I found myself just wanting the day to end.

A few days after Jacob's birthday, I told my family about the requests I'd been receiving to make a recording of "What a Beautiful Name." My parents were just as uncertain about doing it as I was. Almost two months had passed since Jacob's funeral, and the pain was still so fresh. Making a recording seemed inconsequential. But the requests kept coming until we could no longer ignore the idea. We took the decision to God because we couldn't make it on our own. In those days, making even simple decisions felt impossible. For something like this, we needed Father God to tell us what to do.

After a week of praying about it, my parents, Liz, and I had a family meeting to share what God had been revealing to each of us.

"What do you believe we should do here, Anne?" my mom asked.

"It's hard to imagine doing this," I said. "It will be so painful. And I definitely don't feel qualified." I paused before going on. "But I feel the peace of God every time I pray about it. That peace is how He most consistently leads me and how I knew to sing for Jacob's funeral. I think we're supposed to do it."

"Well, so do I," Daddy said. Liz and Mom quickly agreed. It was unanimous—we all felt the Lord leading us to say yes.

"This will be a way for us to look back and see God's faithfulness to us," Mom added.

"I don't know what God wants to do through this video," I said, "but it's obvious He wants us to make it."

Once we heard from God, we went straight to work. We wanted to obey immediately. Looking back, I see that our quick response to the Lord's leading allowed us to capture the purity of the moment, so much like the day of the funeral. In the depths of fresh grief, worship was still the most consistent comfort I found—and that emotion was evident in the finished product.

On the day we would film, I awoke with a sense of foreboding. I was worried the pain of singing the song again would be too great. A song can instantly transport you back to a moment in time, and I feared I might be overtaken by painful memories of Jacob's funeral.

That afternoon, I climbed the narrow stairs to the upper

gathering room of a local ice cream shop. In the old building that had been recently renovated, the upstairs of the shop kept the feel of its history with exposed brick and old wooden benches. Light poured in through floor-to-ceiling windows. Sitting on one of the pew-like benches that surrounded the room, I took in the warmth of the atmosphere there. The rough-hewn floors, the familiarity of a church pew, the sunshine on my face—all of this felt right. More importantly, I felt comforted by the peace of God filling that room. The day promised to hold great pain for me, but as I sat there, sensing His presence, I knew God would uphold me.

A few minutes after I arrived, I was joined by Carson and Hayes, the friends who had played along with me at the funeral. They had agreed to help. Mrs. Powell, Hayes's mom and our family photographer, came to comfort and support my mom. (Mrs. Powell was also the science teacher who had ignited my love for space in seventh grade.)

The air began to fill with the sounds of Carson tuning her violin. Hayes picked the strings of his guitar, warming up his instrument. Liz, who agreed to play the keyboard for me, fought to keep her composure as she ran through the chord progressions. I stood in the middle of it all, dressed in my lacy white blouse, readying myself to sing my song of praise. As we prepared for our first run-through, my mother was overcome with emotion and fled the room in tears; it would be the first of many times that day. Now all I had to do was sing the words to a song that simultaneously broke my heart and healed it.

Paxton, Hayes's older brother and our videographer, showed

me where to stand and readied his equipment. I took deep cleansing breaths as Paxton got Elizabeth into position. Her face held a look of calm determination, but I could see the pain in my sister's eyes. Seeing her hurting so badly cut me to the core. I knew this was a great sacrifice for her.

As the first notes of the song began to play, I was instantly back at the funeral. Yet I was not overwhelmed. Instead, I felt gratitude and awe. *Wow. I can't believe I've made it through the first three months after losing Jacob,* I thought. *God is carrying me through what felt impossible to survive.* My mind flashed to those first moments after learning of Jacob's death, when God promised me He would give us everything we needed to survive. *He's doing it!* I smiled inside as I began to sing praises to my sweet Jesus.

There was deep pain there that day, in that upper room, but there was also surpassing peace. I even felt joy at times. God's presence was thick around us, and I felt the comforting presence of the Almighty. After we finished the final take of the song, I let out a great sigh of relief. We had done it. We had obeyed God and completed this heavy task. He could use it however He chose. I'd done my part, and the rest was in His hands.

On September 12, 2017, we uploaded the video to YouTube for friends and family to watch. My wish, and that of my family, was that it be extremely clear that this video was not about me. The song was dedicated to the memory of my big brother and was intended to honor my Jesus. Beyond that, I had no expectations of it being anything more than a sweet remembrance.

Surprise Message

"Mom?! You've got to see this." I walked briskly through the high school gym, extending my phone in her direction. "What in the world?"

I was now a sophomore, and it was the end of an exhausting day of school. The days were growing shorter as we neared the end of November. Christmas was on the horizon—our first without Jacob. Simply making it through each day was a grueling endeavor.

I had just retrieved my phone from the front desk, where I checked it in each morning before class. As I scrolled through my missed notifications, I came across an Instagram message from a man named Sadi, claiming to be a talent scout.

"What is it, honey?" My mom broke away from her conversation with a teacher to see what was wrong.

I showed her the message, and her look turned to surprise. "What? Who is this? When did you get this?"

"I don't know!" I said. "It came today while I was in class. Do you think this is for real?"

We were skeptical as we read the message. Sadi said he was a talent scout for a manager for Christian music artists in Nashville. He'd seen my video on YouTube and, with our permission, wanted to send it to a manager.

"How did he see it?" Mom asked. We knew the video had been viewed hundreds of times, but we had no idea it had circulated outside our sphere of loved ones.

"I don't know," I said, shaking my head. "This is crazy."

That evening, we showed the message to my dad. "It's probably a scam," I said. *But what if it's God?*

"Let's check this guy out," Daddy said.

A preliminary online search revealed that Sadi was, in fact, a talent scout. He also represented himself as a man who loved God. With my parents' permission and oversight, I replied to the message and requested a phone call.

In the weeks between the message and the phone call, I began to doubt my decision to take this step. Were we doing the right thing in even considering a conversation? Would people think I had used the video to gain recognition or a leg up in the music industry? That thought made me ill. I knew it wasn't true, but even the possibility that it could be perceived that way made me second-guess my decision to talk with Sadi. I didn't want to do anything to dishonor God or Jacob. And still, I had God's words in the back of my mind: music would be my profession.

On the day the call was scheduled, my mom and I ended up needing to run errands. We pulled into a movie theater parking lot to take the call. My phone rang, and I answered it on speakerphone.

"Hi, Anne!" came Sadi's cheerful voice. Mom and I leaned in to hear every word as he listed his credentials and began telling us about Jason, the manager he represented. It was surreal. *There's no way this can be happening,* I thought. *Is this even real?*

"Before I pass your video on to Jason," Sadi said, "I need to know if you are even open to considering a music career. If you aren't, I won't waste Jason's time."

I looked up at my mom and could see the question in her eyes. It was the same question in my own mind. Could I actually do this? I hesitated to say yes because we knew nothing about the music industry. And yet excitement bubbled up inside me. Maybe God wanted to do something amazing through this. As all those mixed emotions coursed through my body, I felt something else. Something deeper. A familiar peace settled in my heart. I nodded at my mom, and she nodded back.

"Yes, Sadi," I finally replied. "I am open to considering a career in music. I'm okay with you passing on the video to Jason."

"That's great!" he said. "I'll be in touch with you soon to let you know what he thinks."

A few days later, we received a text that said Jason was interested and wanted to meet with me. We agreed to set up a time after the new year to visit Nashville and meet with Jason. We would at least explore this opportunity that had just fallen into my lap. But before that meeting, I would have to endure one of the hardest days of my life.

Bitter December

Barely half a year after losing Jacob, we faced our first Christmas without him. Being at our home for Christmas Day without Jacob was too difficult to even consider. We couldn't bear to decorate the house or face the memories of so many happy Christmas mornings together. So, on Christmas Eve, we loaded up and drove the four and a half hours to Asheville, North Carolina.

We'd always wanted to visit the historic Biltmore Estate, built between 1889 and 1895. We decided we'd spend Christmas Day viewing the massive home and gardens of the estate to take our minds off Jacob.

Even during the drive down, we keenly felt Jacob's absence. The car had far too much extra room. I thought back to all the road trips we used to take as a family, piled into one small SUV. Jacob was allowed to sit in the front with Daddy because of his height, and he would lay his seat *all the way back* on Elizabeth and me and try to sleep. Oh, we got so aggravated at him! Whenever I'd finally had enough, I'd ask Mom for permission to pull his hair, and she'd gladly grant it. I'd grab a handful of his dark hair and yank as hard as I could. But Jacob would barely notice. He'd usually just keep his eyes closed, and every now and then he'd laugh at my attempt to punish him. But he never got mad. And now I wished that I was tightly squeezed into a car as he reclined his seat on me, rather than sitting in the back seat with plenty of leg room.

Instead of distracting us, being at the Biltmore only highlighted the massive hole in our family. Laughing children and ornate Christmas decorations filled the immense hallways and rooms. Even leaving our hotel that morning had been triggering. Happy families crowded together in the lobby, opening gifts while Christmas music played on the grand piano. A huge fire roared in the fireplace, but walking through that room left us feeling cold and empty.

Once we arrived at the Biltmore Estate, we did a self-guided tour and listened to the history of the house through earbuds.

As we walked through the house, we became increasingly irritated with each other and began to argue over the most ridiculous things.

"This room is the most beautiful of the whole house," Mom declared as we walked into the banquet hall with its seventy-foot-high ceiling and its massive triple fireplaces.

We'd already seen many of the Biltmore's 250 rooms, and something about my mom's decisive claim irked me. "No, it isn't," I retorted. "This one is definitely *not* the most beautiful."

"Well, which one is then?" she challenged.

"I don't know," I snapped. "And I don't care." I turned away angrily. In our grief, we were starting to turn on each other and melt down over the most insignificant details.

When the tour was over, we trekked through the frigid cold to our car without even trying to view the rest of the grounds.

"We need to find somewhere to eat lunch," Dad said.

"Nothing is open," Liz said resentfully. "It's Christmas Day."

"Yes, I know," Dad returned. "But we need to eat. Let's go to the Stable Cafe here on the estate grounds. At least that's open."

So we ate our Christmas lunch at the Stable Cafe, which would have been a delightful experience under ordinary circumstances. But that day, nothing could please us. We ate in silence, my food tasting like cardboard. Our attempts to find any sort of solace on Christmas Day had failed miserably. Nothing could distract us from our loss and how wrong the holiday felt without Jacob.

We left the restaurant and proceeded to argue over where to go next. Mom wanted to visit a gift shop, but Liz and I just wanted to leave. Dad pulled over in a Wendy's parking lot, where we ended up having a total breakdown. We sat for what felt like forever and just cried.

Nobody put words to what we were feeling, but we all felt it. We were searching for comfort in places we would never find it. We were longing for something that was no longer possible for us to have—our whole family together. And as we sank deeper into our despair, the unspoken thought on each of our minds was that the only person who could pull our family out of this spiral was Jacob. He was always the positive one. But he wasn't there to tease us into laughter or coax smiles to our faces. As hard as we had tried to escape that reality, we had failed.

"What's wrong with us?" I finally said through my tears. "We're fighting about everything."

"I don't know." Mom barely managed the words through her sobs.

"Let's just go back to Lexington," Daddy said. "I can't take any more of this."

As we made the drive home, things only got worse. For a while we stopped speaking to each other. Then we would argue about the most trivial things, like whether we should stop for dinner. Each argument lapsed into another painful silence. At one point I tried to be the peacemaker to end the fighting, but to no avail.

As I pleaded for the fighting to stop, our car approached a bridge, high above sharp rocks and rushing water. That murky water would be very cold this time of year. I stopped talking as a dark thought invaded my mind. It must have hit my mom at the same moment, because we both said, "Why don't we just drive off this bridge right now?"

"We could end our misery," I said.

"We could see Jacob today," Mom whispered.

The words hung in the air. None of us dared speak or move under the weight of them. No one disagreed with the idea or argued against it. We seemed to be in silent, horrified agreement: *This is too hard. Let's just be done.* As the car began to cross the bridge, I thought, *This is it. This is the end.*

Suddenly, words pierced my mind: *No. Do* not *do this.* My head jerked up, and I looked around to see that the rest of my family was also beginning to object. My mom's hand flew to her face, and she frantically shook her head. My dad gripped the steering wheel with determination and kept the car headed in a straight line across the bridge.

"We can't do this," my mom said. "God doesn't want us to do this!"

None of us had audibly heard the voice of God, but we had all felt the same urgent restraint at the exact same time. We could *not* drive off that bridge. It wasn't our time to leave earth and see Jacob. In my spirit, I felt God confirm the words I'd heard from Him a few months earlier—He still had plans for me. I had not yet done all He had created me to do. None of us had. God had not taken us home, so He was not done with us here. And although I had imagined taking things into my own hands and ending my suffering, I knew I needed to trust God. I would have to wait for my reunion with Jacob. I sighed—not with relief but with resignation—and leaned my head against the window. Outside my window, the barren trees and the dead vines that clung to them flew by me as we drove along I-40, a constant reminder of death.

The rest of our drive was very quiet. We were all reeling from what we had just considered, and we were lost in our own thoughts. Back at home, the silence hung heavy between us. What words could anyone say on such a day? With empty souls and bellies, Mom and I went to Texas Roadhouse for dinner, while Daddy and Liz retreated to their separate rooms and shut their doors.

Even in such an innocuous place as a chain restaurant, Mom and I could not escape the pain. A sweet family sat near our table, chattering about their joyful Christmas Day and the gifts they'd received. It was too much to bear. With meals barely touched, we got up from our table and rushed from the restaurant.

On the way home, the silence was only broken by our occasional breathy shudders. I had reached my breaking point and knew I needed to reach out for help. I didn't like to show my weakness, but at that point it didn't matter—I was overwhelmed with grief. Alone in the back seat, as Mom drove toward home, I pulled out my phone. I was desperate for something, anything to ease this relentless, stabbing pain in my heart. I texted a quick plea for help to someone I knew would understand: Lane. Lane, Pastor Cameron's nephew who had lost his dad to a car accident, had been there for me that first week after Jacob died. Lane had convinced me that I would survive this tragedy. He'd been a source of comfort ever since. After seeing my text, he called me immediately.

"Hi Lane," I answered. I had no other words.

"Anne, what's going on?" he asked. The compassion in his voice made me choke up. I managed to get out a few words about how horrible I was feeling. And soon the details of the entire day poured out.

"I just don't know what to do," I finished. "I can't handle this pain anymore. I need help."

"It's okay," Lane said gently. "I understand how that feels."

I understand. Those were the words I desperately needed to hear. Lane continued: "Anne, it might feel impossible for you to endure any more pain, but it's so important for you to realize that God will carry you through this. As hard as it is right now, it *will* get easier. You *will* see God working it for your good. Be patient, Anne. I promise you."

Because I knew he was speaking from experience, I dared to believe him. He ended by praying for me and my whole family. His words and his prayer brought a measure of peace to my soul for the first time that Christmas Day.

By the time the call was over, we were back home. When I hung up, I realized Mom had stayed in the car with me.

"Was that Lane?" she asked. I nodded. "What did he think about our struggle today?"

"He said that he understood and we'd be okay," I said. "I couldn't see past the pain of this day, but he gave me hope that things will get better. I've been trying so hard to hold us all together today, but I couldn't. I just needed help."

As Mom and I sat in the car, we decided we needed to surrender our pain to Jesus all over again. It was too much for us to bear alone. We felt peace after we did, but it was a choice we would have to make again every single day.

New Beginnings

What a relief the new year brought me. The days began to lengthen, and the sun shone a little longer each day. Just the thought of spring renewed my hope. Kentucky is beautiful in the spring. White cherry blossom petals rain down, bright yellow goldenrod bushes brighten yards, and green fields are alive with wobbly-legged foals. I anticipated the joy of seeing new life come out of the dead of winter and hoped to see the same in my own heart.

With the start of 2018 came our meeting with Jason in Nashville. On January 4, we loaded up the car and headed south for the next day's meeting. My nervous excitement intensified with each passing mile. What was I about to walk into? What would come of this meeting?

I had been to Nashville a few times in my life, usually passing through on our way to vacation in Florida. On one such trip, a few summers earlier, we had stopped in Nashville for a quick pit stop at a little coffee and doughnut shop. Daddy, Jacob, and I went in together, and as soon as I set foot in that shop, I felt an unexpected sense of peace. The feeling was so noticeable that it stopped me in my tracks. *Why do I feel so content right now?* I wondered. *What is it about this place that brings me peace?* I looked around but said nothing.

The morning of January 5, I stepped into Jason's office. Immediately, I felt the same sense of peace as I'd experienced in that doughnut shop. There was something about this place—this city—that just felt so right to me. I wondered what it meant and if God were leading me, but mostly I was grateful to feel peace in what could have been a stressful moment.

My parents and I sat in that meeting for six hours. Jason said he thought I had potential to be a successful contemporary Christian music artist. He loved my sound and worshipful style. He was also brutally honest about what it took to be a music artist and the work it required.

"Even in the Christian music world, it takes a lot of effort to make it," he said. "Just because you are singing to the Lord doesn't make the work any easier. This takes an enormous amount of sacrifice."

He went on to talk about the voice lessons and coaching I'd need, what it was like to spend weeks on the road, traveling from city to city, and the effort required just to get one single ready for release. Next, he laid out the money we'd need for start-up costs. After asking countless questions and absorbing a ton of information, we stood to leave. We thanked Jason for his candor and time.

Back in the car, my dad spoke first. "There is no way that this will ever happen," he said. "I mean, that guy is crazy if he thinks we can do all that."

"It does seem impossible," my mom said. She turned to look at Daddy. "Unless God does a miracle, we could never afford it. All the costs for lessons, manager fees, and travel—it's too much for us."

As I listened to them discuss all the requirements Jason had mentioned that day, I felt overwhelmed. I knew the *only* way this would ever come to pass was through the hand of God. My dad had been out of work for almost three months, so money was tight. I was young and still so broken from losing Jacob. The whole idea seemed improbable.

"You're right, Mom," I said. "It would take a move of God." We would have to be utterly confident that God was leading me down this path to justify the costs. "If God's not in it, it's not worth considering. I only go if He says go."

That's where we left it as we drove home to Kentucky. There was no decision to make—just the realization that the only way a future in the music industry would happen was if God made a way where there seemed to be no way. That was good with me. I couldn't make this happen on my own and knew it would be pointless to try.

Singing "What a Beautiful Name" at Jacob's funeral and recording a video of the song had never been my idea. I didn't go looking for a manager. God had initiated and directed me in all of it. If He were the Author of this story, why would I ever try to take the pen? In that moment, I determined I would not make a move without His direct confirmation. I would wait and see what Jesus would do. If this were part of God's plan for me, He would make it happen. And if it weren't, I knew He had something else in store. As Lane had reminded me in my lowest moment, He was working all things for my good.

A Note from Anne

When I was walking through the grief of losing Jacob, there were days I wanted to give up. There were days that seemed more difficult than I could bear. If God had not been with me every step of the journey, I don't know how I would have survived. The pain was too much for just me. But thank God, it was never *just me.* My Immanuel was with me, and He's with you too.

Here is what I learned: When the pain, memories, and what-ifs overwhelm you, surrender them to God. Take every thought captive to the truth (2 Corinthians 10:5). Give God what you yourself cannot bear. Picture yourself handing it over, giving Him your heart, and falling into His embrace. Do this again and again and again. When you're in a place of grief or lingering depression, every day feels like climbing out of a pit of despair. The way out is not through your own strength, but through surrendering to God and allowing Him to lift you out. When I accepted that losing Jacob was a tragedy too great for me and out of my control—when I chose to trust God even though nothing made sense—that is when I felt relief. I invite you to release your pain and struggles into God's hands and trust Him. It's one of the great paradoxes of God: only when we surrender do we become free.

> Cast all your care upon Him, because He cares for you.
>
> 1 PETER 5:7 MEV

EIGHT

A God-Sized Dream

I RETURNED FROM MY MEETING IN NASHVILLE BACK TO normal life in Kentucky. Classes resumed and were a welcome distraction. My mom busied herself leading the school, and Elizabeth poured herself into building her clothing company. Liz had been growing her home-based business for the previous four years, after opening an Etsy shop when she was sixteen. For three years, she sold her hand-sewn designs through her shop. As her colorful Southern apparel continued to sell out quickly, Liz knew she needed to expand production and manufacturing and work from her own web platform. She had begun work on a website in the spring of 2017.

Then we lost Jacob, and like all of us, she wanted to give up. But the Lord guided Liz in the opposite direction. Two months after we lost Jacob, Liz launched her website in his honor. Her business had been steadily growing ever since. And now Daddy began volunteering his time to help her take it to the next level.

We kept trudging through the day-to-day of living because we didn't have a choice. Some days were easier than others, but each one was painful. To an outsider, we probably looked like a normal family, but in truth, we remained in survival mode.

The next three months were a season of waiting for me. I questioned what my future held and kept expecting God to show me a clear sign. But the sign never came. I dreaded the upcoming summer months, which brought with them reminders of losing Jacob—the anniversary of his death in June and his birthday in August. I focused on anything that would distract me from these thoughts. I stayed diligent with my schoolwork, and I began researching colleges and music programs that might be options for me after I graduated.

Since a music career in Nashville seemed unlikely, I set my mind on finding an alternate path to follow God's call into music. But I felt like I was spinning my wheels. As I sought God for answers, none came. So far God had not provided a way for me to pursue being a music artist, and I wondered if He had an entirely different route in mind for me.

With spring in full bloom and the end of my sophomore year quickly approaching, I decided I should take some steps toward a decision. I love a plan, and I wanted one in place before summer. Deciding on a course of action felt safer to me, as it always does.

One breezy April day, I came home from school and went straight to my room to call Erica, Pastor Cameron's wife. I knew she would give me wise counsel. She had become a close confidante and mentor to me in recent years, and even more so since I had lost Jacob.

"Hey, Anne!" Erica answered. "Is everything okay?"

"Yes, I'm okay," I reassured her. "I just needed to talk to you for a bit. I'm really struggling with knowing which direction to go with music and worship. I'm not at all sure what God wants me to do."

"Okay," she said. "Tell me what's going on."

"Well, I have no peace when I research colleges," I said, "but the idea of going to a worship program I found out in California sounds perfect to me."

"What do your parents think?" Erica asked.

"They're okay with me not attending college if God is calling me elsewhere, but they aren't thrilled about the idea of my going out to California." I paused for a moment. "And then, of course, we all have the idea of pursuing a music career in Nashville floating around in our heads. That's exciting and scary for me to think about. I'm so new to all this—do I even have what it takes to make it in Nashville?"

"So, what is God saying to *you*, Anne?" Erica asked the exact question I knew we would land on.

"That's just it," I said. "He's been pretty quiet lately. I don't know what He wants me to do . . . ." My voice trailed off as my mind began to spin. *Why was God so quiet when I needed such critical direction?*

"What is your heart's desire, Anne?" Erica's voice pulled me back from my thoughts.

"I want to be in a place where I can grow in the Lord," I answered. "I want to lead authentic worship and influence the kingdom of God." This part I knew.

"Your heart is in the right place," Erica said. "God knows all your desires and has your best interests in mind. He promises in His Word to give you the desires of your heart—even if He accomplishes that in a different way than you had in mind. I *know* He will do it. You can trust Him."

I let Erica's words sink in.

"And, Anne," she added, "it's so important to honor your parents in all this, so if they have reservations about your going out to California, you can trust that God will bless you for honoring them."

Later, as I thought about all Erica had said, I knew her advice was sound, even if it was difficult. My heart was set on going out to California, and the idea of pursuing a music career in Nashville felt daunting. The most immediate hurdle was the financial requirement to even get started. If God wanted me in a music career, He would have to provide.

That May, about a month after my conversation with Erica, I woke up one morning with a dream playing at the edges of my mind. As I sat sleepy-eyed in my bed, I wrapped my arms around my knees and closed my eyes tightly, trying to remember. Suddenly the details of the dream flashed through my mind.

I was standing in a recording studio in Nashville with my parents and Jason. The studio was dimly lit, and I sensed there was also a producer in the room with us whom I couldn't see. Then I heard the voice of God speak to me in the dream: "The money will come on August 1." Then the dream ended.

I immediately knew the dream was from God, intended to

guide me toward the path of a career in Nashville. I wrote the dream down in my journal and jumped up to go tell my mom.

"Mom!" I called. "You won't believe the dream I just had." I ran downstairs to find her sipping her morning coffee in the kitchen. I quickly described my dream.

"Honey, that's amazing!" Mom said with a smile. "And that will be incredible if that's what God wants to do." She may not have been fully convinced that my dream was from God, but I most certainly was. In my mind, God had just confirmed the path He desired me to walk.

Months of Remembering

With the warm days of summer came the one we all dreaded—June 7, the one-year anniversary of Jacob's death. We decided to be away from home the entire week so we wouldn't be surrounded by the familiar places where we'd shared the worst day of our lives. We headed to the beach, hoping the warmth of the sun and constancy of the ocean would give us some peace.

After surviving our first year without Jacob, my mom had the idea to host a night where we could gather with loved ones to remember him. She began to plan a memorial evening for mid-July and asked me to lead worship for the evening. We found out that two other families in our town had recently lost a son, so we invited them to join us to honor all three young men. We invited anyone who had experienced grief to attend.

Pastor Cameron and Erica graciously offered to host the evening at the large barn on their property. "The Barn," as we call it, sits high on a hill south of Lexington. From the back barn doors you can see for miles, right into the heart of the city. That night, I stood at those doors before the service began and relaxed into the beauty of the evening.

It was a perfect night. Hot and humid, as Kentucky summers are, but gorgeous. Green trees filled the landscape below, and soft clouds dotted the sky. Birds flitted at eye level from one tree to another, and a gentle breeze kissed my face.

Tonight is for you, Jacob, I whispered in my heart. *And it's for You, my Jesus. As I worship, please draw hurting hearts to Yourself. May people turn their faces to You and give You their pain. Do for them what You did for me that first night when Jacob died.*

I felt a sad calm in my spirit as I finished praying, but no fear of leading worship. I was grateful for this opportunity and hopeful for what God would do. I also ached for my brother. Reminders of his funeral and the hole in my life left by his absence reawakened. I wasn't overwhelmed by the emotions, but they were heavy upon me.

Hundreds of people came that night until every chair we had rented was full. I walked up to the keyboard for worship, with Carson and Hayes once again by my side. The stunning view into Lexington was behind us, leaving us backlit to the point that no one could see our faces. That was perfect. I wanted all the focus to be on the Lord.

I chose songs that I had worshiped with often over the past

year, in the hope they would minister hope and healing to those who needed it. I sang "Confident" by Steffany Gretzinger and "You're Gonna Be Okay" by Jenn Johnson. Stoic faces softened as those in the crowd were led into the presence of God.

When I started singing "What a Beautiful Name," sounds of weeping mixed in with the sounds of our worship. *You're doing it, God,* I thought. *You are turning their faces back to You and letting me be a part of it. You are so endlessly good.*

Once worship was over, families shared memories of their lost loved ones, and Pastor Cameron delivered a message about the hope we have in Jesus to see our loved ones again. At the end we offered a prayer time, and it felt like nearly everyone in the place came forward to be prayed over. As people finally began to leave and the last few were receiving prayer, the three families went outside to light floating luminaries in memory of the young men we had lost.

I wrote a private message to Jacob on mine and sent it into the sky. The luminary floated up and over the hills, toward the bright lights of Lexington. I watched until the lantern was a pinpoint of light on the horizon. Throughout the night my spirit felt alive. I knew leading people to the throne of God, where they could release their burdens, was what I was made to do.

A week after the memorial, I sat on my bed reading my Bible before going to sleep. This had come to be a comforting place, cocooned in my soft blankets with the Word of God open before me. I expected God to meet me here, and He did. As I read the Word that night, I came to Psalm 59:16–17:

> But I will sing of Your power;
> I will sing aloud of Your lovingkindness in the
> morning,
> for You have been my refuge
> and escape in the day of my trouble.
> To You, O my strength, I will sing,
> for God is my refuge, and the God of my
> lovingkindness. (MEV)

I read the words again, letting them sink into my soul. I began to pray this psalm back to God. *God, it's true—every morning is a blessing because You renew Your mercies and hope to me as the sun rises afresh each day,* I said. *You truly are the One I run to for protection and help. I've had so many days of trouble, but You have been my strength through them all. I'm ready, God, to tell the world how faithful You are. I will sing to You for all You've done.*

As I prayed, soft worship music played on the radio. The song playing caught my attention. The words of "Let It Happen" by United Pursuit filled the room, and the lyrics encouraged me to surrender everything to God and let Him do the work. I turned the words of the song back to God.

Father, if You want me to begin a music career in Nashville, let it happen, I prayed. *If this is what You want, then let it happen.* The dream I'd had two months earlier came to my mind. I had felt so confident then that God was confirming the path to Nashville with that dream. It was still up to Him to fulfill it, but I wanted to give Him my full yes. I did my very best to put the situation into His hands and believe *He* would fulfill His plans for me.

Marveling at how God had orchestrated such a beautiful moment of surrender for me, I paused to write a note in my Bible next to that scripture: "A day of prayer for Nashville, praying over it. Let it happen, Lord."

God's Provision

Three days later, on a Wednesday afternoon, Daddy walked into the kitchen with the mail in his hand. He came over to the table where I was seated in front of my laptop and stood there until I looked up. He kept a straight face, but I could tell he was about to burst with some news.

"Here you go, Anne," he said, holding out an envelope he had opened moments earlier.

I took the envelope and pulled out its contents. I stared at a check made out to me from my Granddaddy with almost the exact amount we needed to hire a manager.

"What is this?!" I said, my hand flying to my mouth. "Daddy, are you serious?" Tears started running down my cheeks as I laughed and cried at the same time. I kept looking back and forth between Daddy and the miracle in my hand. My earthly father had handed me the check, and his father had written it, but I knew immediately my heavenly Father was the One who had supplied it.

"It's real, Anne," he said, smiling. "And it's almost everything you need to sign with a manager."

"This is too good to be true," I said, burying myself in my

daddy's embrace. Then I pulled back quickly. "Where's Mom? We've got to show her!"

I ran into my parents' bedroom, waving the check in the air like I'd just won the lottery. "Mom! You won't believe what God just did!"

My tears continued to flow as I showed my mom the check. We cried together, overwhelmed with gratitude. Suddenly, I stopped and reached into my pocket to pull out my phone. I looked at the date.

"It's August 1," I said. "Mom! Daddy! Today is August 1, just like in my dream!"

At that moment, I had no doubt about God's will for me. This miraculous provision came through the generous gift of my Granddaddy, Daddy's father, out of his desire to invest in all his grandchildren. No one outside our immediate family had any idea I was even considering a music career. For ten months, we had kept the possibility just between our little family and God. Never before had I received a gift like this from anyone, and now it arrived on the exact date God had revealed His provision would come. I looked down at the check once again and knew it marked the beginning of a new chapter in my life.

When Liz arrived home that evening, I ran down the stairs to meet her at the door and tell her my news. She hugged me, overjoyed by how God had provided. Her next words took me by surprise.

"Anne, don't worry about the rest of the money," she said. "I'm going to supply the remaining amount so you can immediately start with your manager."

My chin quivered. "You are?" I asked. Liz nodded her head. My sister's generosity was almost too much. I felt undeserving. I wrapped my arms around my sister and held on tightly. "Thank you, Liz. Thank you. I love you so much."

Liz had decided to invest some of her company's profits in me. Her contribution brought me right to the amount I needed to sign with Jason. I don't miss the beauty in the fact that my sister's realized dreams allowed her to launch me into mine. I'm so proud of her. She has been an example to me of perseverance. She has allowed suffering to make her stronger.

With the funds miraculously in hand, we stepped out in faith and signed with Jason as my manager in August 2018. I intentionally say "we stepped out" because it was not just me who was risking here. My whole family was stepping out in faith with me and were willing to invest time, money, and hard work right alongside me. Ever since Jacob, Liz, and I were children, the Wilsons had been supporting and playing a part in one another's dreams. Even at ten when I started "Anne's Camp," it was evident my family would be right there with me, no matter what I put my hand to.

Steps of Obedience

Right from the start, I saw that Jason was right; pursuing a career as a Christian music artist required tremendous work. He advised me to begin taking vocal lessons immediately, which I did. To maintain longevity in the business, I needed to learn how to protect and strengthen my vocal cords. While I prepared for next steps, Jason also suggested I start leading worship and offering to sing at churches every opportunity I got. I needed to get in the habit of being onstage and leading others in song.

After our memorial evening in July, Pastor Cameron approached me with an idea. He offered the Barn as a venue for me to start a ministry for high school and college students. I jumped at the chance. Leading this ministry would allow me to pursue my heart for authentic worship and gain the onstage experience I needed. Our "Barn Nights" were birthed out of that special evening of remembering Jacob, which will always make them dear to my heart.

On Sunday evenings, starting in September and continuing through the school year, we gathered at the Barn for worship, teaching, and prayer. I distributed flyers at school and youth group to get the word out. I was excited to lead an intimate worship experience and see students transformed through the Word and prayer. Those who came seemed as hungry as I was for a deeper experience with God. At their height, those worship nights grew to around seventy-five students. I discovered I could rely on feeling God's peace and presence every time I led worship. God was building my confidence—not in my own ability but in His ability to bring to pass the promises He made to me.

Launching

My phone buzzed repeatedly on the desk next to me as I sat working on my homework. It was the second semester of my junior year, and my workload had greatly increased. As I tried to remain focused on my French assignment, my buzzing phone stole my attention. I finally put down my pen and reached for it. *Whoever is texting must have something important to say,* I thought.

All the messages were from my manager, Jason, who told me it was time to start planning a writing trip to Nashville. He told me to expect to be there for a week, and he would schedule a different writing session for each business day. *Five writing sessions in one week?* My stomach flip-flopped at the thought. I headed straight down to the kitchen to find my parents.

"Jason says it's time to begin writing music down in Nashville," I blurted. Mom and Daddy looked at me. Was that curiosity or fear in their eyes?

"Oh my . . . . When does that begin, and what do we need to do?" Moving from surprise to action never took Mom very long.

"He wants to send me on a writing trip, and his assistant is going to call us and set it all up," I said. Even as I spoke those words, my voice shook a little. Self-doubting thoughts raced through my mind. *I'm not a writer. I've never written a song in my life! How in the world can I do this?*

Daddy must have heard the uncertainty in my voice because he pulled me into an embrace.

"I feel scared," I admitted. "I don't know if I'm ready for this."

"Well, we'll take it one step at a time," Daddy said. "If it's God's will, it'll work out." My father always had a way centering me. He was right, of course. If God got me into this whole thing, He would carry me through it.

In April 2019, Mom and I drove down to Nashville. I had

to explain to my teachers and friends at school why I would be absent for a whole week. We'd been trying to keep the entire situation as under wraps as possible, but it couldn't remain private much longer. I had to be honest about where I was going and why I was missing school. My going on a songwriting trip to Nashville must have sounded odd to my friends. I could hardly believe it myself.

On Monday morning, Mom drove me over to East Nashville to the address Jason had given us. Thanks to my need for punctuality, we arrived twenty minutes early. I started to gather my things when Mom said, "Honey, you don't need to walk in twenty minutes before they're expecting you. We should just sit here and wait for a little bit."

"You're right," I conceded. "But can we find a place to pray together first? I'm feeling pretty nervous." Mom pulled back onto the road and found a Walgreens nearby where she parked, and we prayed together.

When we'd finished praying, Mom looked at me expectantly.

"Okay, Mom, I'm good to go," I said.

A few minutes later, we arrived back at the little modern gray house. I turned to say goodbye to my mom. I could see the fear in her eyes.

"What about you, Mom?" I asked. "Are *you* good?"

"I'll be fine," she said. "Just feeling protective of my baby girl. I feel like I'm dropping you off for your first day of kindergarten." I later learned that my mom had been quite nervous to let me go in alone, but my manager had assured her that these men were well-known in the Christian music industry and personally vetted by him.

I assured her I would be fine, hugged her goodbye, and hopped out of the car. I had to face this on my own, and I dug deep for the courage to ring that doorbell. The man who answered the door introduced himself as Jeff Sojka, the producer I'd be working with that day. He led me to the studio at the back of the house where the writer, Matt Armstrong, was waiting for us. I sat down nervously on a white couch. Matt sat in a chair while Jeff took a seat at his producer's table. We spent a little bit of time getting to know one another, and then Matt looked at me and tilted his head slightly.

"We can tell you are nervous," he said with a smile, nodding toward my hands. "Your hands are shaking."

"Oh, yes," I said with a nervous laugh. "I've never done this before. I don't know what to expect."

"Don't worry." He smiled again. "It'll be okay. We will walk you through the process."

Matt and Jeff treated me like a friend and set my mind at ease. Their kindness made it easier to open up to them about my life. My story of losing my beloved brother, Jacob, and honoring him through the song in my video was one reason Jason had seen potential in me. The pain I'd walked through, and my heart to share it through music, could provide the inspiration for songs.

Jeff, Matt, and I talked a lot about Jacob that day. I told them how much I missed him every day and longed for our reunion in heaven. By the end of our session, we had cowritten a song called

"In the Waiting" about the time in between losing a loved one and seeing them again in heaven.

As I left, I hugged Matt and Jeff and thanked them for their kindness to me that day. Then I hurried out of the house to find my mom waiting in the car. As I opened the door and slid into my seat, I felt so light and carefree. Before she could even ask how it went, I started verbally downloading the details of my day.

"Mom, these guys were amazing!" I said. "I feel like they are actually my friends now. Today was *so* much fun!"

The rest of my week consisted of writing sessions with various professional songwriters, and I loved every minute of it. I assumed that once I finished this writing trip, Mom and I would head home to Kentucky and spend some time waiting for the next step. But Jason called me the very next day.

"Anne!" he said the moment I answered the phone. "I got a call from the VP of Capitol Christian Music Group. He just finished having lunch with Jeff Sojka, who told him all about you and the song you guys worked on yesterday. And he's interested in you."

"Wait, what?" My mind was racing to catch up with Jason's rush of words. "What do you mean? Who is interested?"

"Jeff had lunch with the VP of Capitol today, Josh Bailey," he repeated. "Josh asked Jeff if he'd been working with any new artists, and he told him about *you*! He showed him the song you guys wrote yesterday, and now Capitol wants to meet with you."

"When?!" I was shocked at the speed at which this was all happening.

"They are asking for you to come back to Nashville next month," Jason said. "You'll participate in more writing sessions and meet with some of the people from Capitol Christian Music. Anne, do you realize what a big deal this is? It *never* happens this fast."

Even though I was astounded by what God was orchestrating so quickly, I don't think I fully grasped how miraculous it was. Looking back after several years in the industry, I have a greater appreciation for the size of mountains God moved on my behalf—and the ones He continues to move.

After one week of writing in Nashville, word about me began to spread. I soon had meetings with multiple labels scheduled for the following month. Throughout that summer, I returned to Music City for a weeklong songwriting trip every month. And by August, I had offers on the table to sign with *three* different record labels.

I was all too aware I was only seventeen and about to make one of the biggest decisions of my life. What God had laid before me now seemed more like a highway than a path. Never in my wildest dreams could I have envisioned this for myself. I couldn't have imagined a dream this big. What was unfolding seemed more incredible to me than my dream of becoming an astronaut. Yet it was happening. I was watching God do the impossible to fulfill His plans for my life.

I think the fact that God brought me three options of record labels to sign with shows how abundant He is in His goodness. He only needed to provide one, but He offered me three. As I surveyed His extravagant provision, I was in awe. But I was also anxious about the decision before me. What if I made a mistake or missed His guidance in deciding which offer to accept? My choice would change my life. But I was not alone in any of it. My parents were always by my side, constantly supporting and protecting me. They trusted that God was at work, showing me the path He had for me. Truly, God did not leave me on my own to make the decision, just as He had not left me alone in my grief over Jacob or the incredible journey I was now on. All I needed to do was keep my eyes on Jesus.

A Note from Anne

Have you ever noticed that God has a way of showing up just in time? He is rarely early, but He is never late. Part of trusting Him is believing He'll show up when we need Him, even if we don't see anything happening. The waiting is hard, though, isn't it? But once you begin to see Him working, it builds your faith for the next time. You can remind yourself: *God did it then, and He'll do it again. I can trust Him.*

I love how God was so kind to reveal to me ahead of time that He would provide the money to hire a manager. When it happened, my confidence in Him blossomed. But as we walk with Him, He leads us into deeper maturity. I don't always get advance notice like I did in that instance. But as I remember all that He has done, both for me personally and throughout Scripture, it fortifies my faith, and I can trust more easily. I can choose to believe that He will make a way for me, even if my circumstances tell me it's impossible. You may not have your answer yet, but don't give up. His timing is perfect, and His provision will be just what you need.

I am confident I will see the Lord's goodness
while I am here in the land of the living.
Wait patiently for the Lord.
Be brave and courageous.
Yes, wait patiently for the Lord.

Psalm 27:13–14 NLT

NINE

Turning Points

I SAT IN MY CAR AS THE RAIN PELTED MY WINDSHIELD. When the light turned green, my car began to creep forward, but my mind was stuck spinning in place. The decision of which label I would sign with loomed before me, and the magnitude of the choice paralyzed me. For weeks I'd been thinking and praying about this decision. I had a detailed pros-and-cons list going and had conducted plenty of research on each label. I had also asked my family members and mentors to join me in seeking the Lord's guidance. After a summer of writing songs in Nashville, September had arrived, and it was time to make my decision.

Every day I brought the three options before the Lord. And each time I prayed about signing with Capitol Christian Music Group, I felt peace. That peace is usually my best indicator of the Lord's guidance, but in this situation, I struggled to trust it. Each label was reputable and had extended a strong offer. None was an obvious front-runner. With three seemingly equal choices, the only big difference was how I felt. But I was worried about trusting my feelings. I was only seventeen and longed for someone to just tell me which label to pick. So I went to my parents to get their wisdom. They had been weighing all the options right alongside me, but they had also encouraged me to listen and follow God's direction for myself.

"Honey," Daddy said, "God has led us every step of the way. I know He'll show us what to do."

"But what if what I'm feeling is just my own emotions and not God's leading?" I asked. "I just want someone to tell me what to do."

"God will tell you, Anne," Mom said. "And we're here to support you. I've watched God answer my cries for direction with my work many times. He sometimes answers at the very last minute, but He's never late, honey."

I thought about my mom's words as I drove home from school through the late-summer rain, but all my confidence in hearing from God seemed to have dissipated in the face of this monumental decision. I feared I would mess up everything if I chose the wrong label. I knew God had already provided for me to be discovered, hire a manager, and learn songwriting, and yet I struggled to rest in *His* ability to handle my present dilemma.

Suddenly I got an idea. I would reach out to someone who would understand exactly what I was facing. I pulled into a parking lot and picked up my phone to call Jeff Pardo. I had met Jeff during my first writing trip to Nashville. He was the writer paired with me on my second day. Within thirty minutes of meeting him, I knew he would be a dear friend. Jeff is married with kids, yet not much older than Jacob would have been. I felt an instant brother-sister connection to Jeff and a freedom to be vulnerable in telling him my story. I shared about losing my brother and the details of that awful night. When I told Jeff my response to God in saying, "Jesus, I trust You," he held up a hand to stop me.

"That's it!" he said. "That's what we're going to write about today." And we did. Within an hour we wrote a song called "I'll Trust You." Inspired by one of the most pivotal moments of my life, that song held deep meaning for me. And I was amazed at what a high level of talent Jeff had to pull the idea from my story so quickly. Jeff was involved in many of my writing sessions over the next few months and had become like a brother to me. So, when I needed some advice that rainy day, I dialed Jeff's number.

"Jeff, what should I do?" I asked after explaining that each label was making a similar appealing offer. "You've been in this industry a long time—what do you think?"

"Anne, listen," Jeff said. "If you had to choose right this second, who would you pick? Don't think about it, just answer from your gut."

"Capitol," I said without hesitating. I sensed the familiar peace again. Instantly I knew this was the answer I'd been looking for. God had been speaking it to me for weeks now, but I'd been too scared of making a mistake to believe I'd heard Him correctly. Jeff's simple question helped me see that God had already answered.

God taught me another vital lesson through that phone call. I'd reached out to my best friend in the industry, one I deeply trusted, to help me know what to do. But instead of telling me what to do, Jeff forced me to be honest about what I already knew inside—what the Lord had already revealed. I realized that to be successful—successful in *my* sense of the word, honoring God and telling the world about Him—I would have to listen to His voice above all others. There would be many voices vying to influence me in the days to come. Some of those people would know a lot more about all of this than I did. And I would probably be tempted to look to them instead of seeking God first.

Then and there, I determined to be humble enough to learn from the experienced and wise people God brought into my life but also to follow God's guidance for my life first and foremost. Ultimately, His opinion of me was the only one that mattered.

Making It Official

Three months later, on December 10, 2019, Mom, Liz, and I stood in the bathroom at the headquarters of Capitol Christian Music Group. We stood in front of the mirror as Mom and Liz helped me make final adjustments to my appearance. I felt zero nervousness for what lay ahead that day—officially signing with Capitol. I felt only thankfulness for how far the Lord had brought me in such a short time.

"I know this is right," I told them as they smoothed my hair and adjusted my blouse. "This is exactly where I'm supposed to be. I feel such a sense of peace and expectancy. God is going to do something beautiful out of all of this. I just know it."

We grabbed each other's hands and squeezed, absorbing the

gravity of the moment together. No one outside our little family could fully appreciate just how much God had brought us through and how far He had led us in such a short time.

I gathered that day with my family and my manager, Jason, and a group of people from Capitol to sign the contract and to celebrate this new partnership. As I sat down to sign my name, with my family by my side, I knew Jesus was by my side as well. I felt His presence. A photographer snapped some pictures to commemorate the signing, and we joined in a reception where I spoke from my heart to everyone present. Capitol had asked me to share a bit of my story and an original song for those who gathered with us that day. After I told them about losing Jacob and being called into music, I opened up about my gratitude for this new relationship.

"I am so grateful to be a part of this company," I said. "The way you at Capitol Christian Music Group have handled this entire process as I chose a label reminds me of Jesus. I have felt the Lord's hand on this the whole time. He has been so faithful to me through all the grief of the past two and a half years. I'm thankful for this opportunity, and I'm looking forward to what the future holds."

I ended by singing the first song I wrote with Jeff Pardo, "I'll Trust You." It seemed the perfect way to honor God for all He had done to lead me to that point. I could see that God was writing an incredible story out of my devastation. As I launched my music career that day, I wanted to tell Jesus again that I trusted Him with my future. And as I did, tears of thankfulness came. My calm exterior broke for a moment, undone by God's faithfulness to me. And it seemed I was only just beginning the journey. Who knew what else God had in store for me?

The Unexpected

At the beginning of 2020, my label and management made plans to release my first single that May. However, I wasn't feeling peace about the timing because we hadn't settled on the right song yet. I didn't want to rush this once-in-a-lifetime opportunity of releasing my first single without having just the right song.

In addition, we had not yet landed on the specific style I would have as an artist. In the music industry, you must commit to a style and sound to help your audience know what they can expect from you. A brand also helps your management and label know how to market you to those who will most appreciate your sound. I did not have a focused sound yet. Suggestions had centered around a youthful pop-artist style or a modern hipster-worship vibe. But neither of these ideas felt authentic to who I am. Still, I had zero ideas for an alternative.

Jason had emphasized the importance of the first single. As the old saying goes, you only get one shot to make that first impression. I needed an authentic sound and the right song before I could release it. Nevertheless, we kept the goal of releasing a song in May, and I continued to work on writing songs, hoping to stumble upon just the right one in time for the release.

The year 2020 also marked my senior year of high school. I was barreling toward the end of my high school career with a sadness that it would all soon be over mixed with anticipation for what lay ahead. In early March, Mom and I, along with Aunt Nene and her daughter and my best friend, Sarah, went on a senior trip to Walt Disney World in Orlando. This girls' trip was the perfect way to celebrate the end of our childhood journey together. Mom and Aunt Nene were graduating their last babies from the school they had founded together eight years earlier. The getaway was not only a celebration of Sarah's and my graduating but also of God fulfilling the dream our moms had to build a school where young minds and hearts could thrive.

As we walked the streets of Disney World on our final day there, we began to hear more news about a virus that had entered our country. A handful of cases of the novel coronavirus had already been confirmed in the United States, and there were rumors of nationwide lockdowns. Throughout the day, my phone kept buzzing with texts from friends, telling me the latest news. When Daddy called, he told Mom about the bare shelves he'd seen at the grocery store. With every new bit of information, my fear grew. I like to know what is going to happen, and this pandemic situation was quickly getting out of control. We were eight hundred miles from home, and I was worried about getting trapped in Florida, far away from Daddy.

We were able to travel home just in time, stepping through our front door just one day before the lockdowns began. As a family, we discussed how we would respond to the crisis.

"It sounds like we'll have to stay home for at least fifteen days," Dad said.

"Can we go out to the farm instead of staying here?" I asked.

"Wouldn't it be better to be out in the country than here in town? We can be there to help Granddaddy and Jan."

"Yes, I love that idea," Mom agreed. "We'll be naturally isolated and in a place we love."

"And we'll be near Jacob's grave," I added. Elizabeth gave me a knowing look and took my hand. Being near Jacob's resting place always gave us comfort. In a season of massive uncertainty, being as near to Jacob as possible felt important. Spending a few weeks at the farm appeared to be the perfect solution for our little family. So we loaded up our luggage and Jacob's dog, Sallie, and headed out to weather the lockdown in our favorite place.

With the nation shutting down, there was no possibility of returning to Nashville anytime soon, which put the release date for my first single on an indefinite hold. I was grateful that we had more time to find the right sound and song, even though it came as the result of such a horrible situation in our world.

We left for the farm with the understanding that we would only stay fifteen days. But six weeks later we were still there. Like other schools in the area, Veritas Christian Academy went virtual for the rest of the school year, so I completed my senior year from my bedroom at the farm. Daddy had become an official employee of Elizabeth's clothing company by this time, and the two of them continued her internet-based business from the farm. Life may have been turned upside down for us, yet it was during those six weeks that God set me firmly on the path that would determine my future.

Every morning out on the Wilson Farm, I rose before the sun was up and took my coffee, Bible, and journal to Jacob's grave. His grave is on a small hill behind Granddaddy's house and barn—a favorite spot of Jacob's when he was alive. We surrounded the spot with a black wooden fence and marked his grave with a beautifully engraved headstone. It reads:

In Loving Memory

Jacob Kent
Wilson

August 21, 1993
June 7, 2017

Blessed is the man who listens to me,
Watching daily at my doorstep,
waiting at my doorway. –Proverbs 8:34

From this raised spot of earth, you can see the sun rise and set in all its glorious beauty. You can look down to Granddaddy's old wooden barn or up to the hill where Jacob and I often shot guns together. This is where I spent my time with the Lord throughout those weeks of uncertainty.

One morning, a few weeks after we'd come to the farm, I walked out to the gravesite to enjoy the sunrise with the Lord. I held my warm cup of coffee in my hands and watched the steam rise with the sun. I felt a heavy weight in my soul. The world's situation with a global pandemic was foremost in my mind and filled me with concern. I prayed for healing, protection, and answers.

My thoughts wandered to the imminent decision about my sound as an artist. I still hadn't settled on a distinct sound and style. Though my label and my management had made suggestions, I needed my Father's guidance. I opened up to the Lord about my worries, telling Him my concerns.

Everyone has ideas for me about what my style should be, I prayed. *But none of them feel right for* me. *I don't want other people determining my course—only You, Jesus. You placed me on this journey, and I trust You to lead me forward in it. Please show me the unique sound You've given me. Give me Your peace.*

After I handed my worries over to the Lord, I had an intense desire to feel closer to Jacob. There's not a moment of any day that goes by when I don't miss him, but sitting there by his grave made me acutely aware of my longing to feel near him. I looked up at the hill where we used to shoot together. I ached to see his smile, hear his voice, and sense his comforting presence. I would have given anything for him to make me laugh just one more time.

I pulled out my phone and turned on some country music. Songs played that Jacob and I had listened to during those sweet drives out to the farm in his truck. Within seconds, the melodies transported me back to our Friday afternoon drives together. As I heard the familiar twang of those voices, I could almost imagine Jacob sitting next to me. One of his favorite songs started, and I stared at his name on the large stone that marked his resting place. Tears rolled down my cheeks. I didn't wipe them away. I welcomed the release that came from being in this place and hearing the music my brother loved. The gravesite was still the one place where I faced Jacob's death and stopped distracting myself from its reality for a brief span of time.

As the notes of the song faded, I had a sudden realization. All at once, I recognized the thread of a Southern country style throughout my entire life. From eating the squirrel meat Jacob prepared for me to catching crawdads to rolling along in a pickup truck with the windows down, blasting country music, I was a Southern girl at heart. And my heart's desire was to worship Jesus. It was as though a veil lifted from my eyes and I saw it clearly for the first time. In that moment, I envisioned country music and Christian worship colliding, and I knew *that* was my sound.

I sensed God speaking to me in my spirit. *This is who you are as an artist,* He said. *This is who I've been building you to be for your whole life.*

Fresh tears fell as I received God's direction with relief and joy. *Of course! This is exactly who I am,* I thought, *and it honors my brother in a beautifully authentic way.* My best moments with Jacob were listening to country music and spending time together out on the farm. I wouldn't have to manufacture this sound. It was already built into the fabric of my being by my Creator God. I just had to let it out and glorify His name through it.

Those six weeks at Granddaddy's were some of the most pivotal days of my life. There, God showed me who He had created me to be as an artist. And during my sunrise worship and prayer times, He gave me ideas for songs that were yet to be written. As an artist, I was expected to generate song concepts and potential titles from my own life experiences. I would bring those titles into writing sessions as the groundwork for songs I would write and sing with other songwriters.

My time with Jesus on the farm produced many song concepts and titles, including "Something About That Name" and "Devil." As I came simply to meet with God, He offered me direction, song ideas, and healing. I showed up. He did the rest.

One morning in April, I rose early for my time with God at the grave. I pulled on a warm sweatshirt because the mornings were still chilly in the hills. As I made my way to the gravesite, I noticed the mist beginning to lift and heard the birds singing their morning songs. The earth was readying itself for a new day, and I could feel the hope of that newness in my soul.

I walked through the wet grass out to Jacob's grave and sipped my coffee as I soaked in the Lord's presence. Once daylight had fully arrived, I opened my journal to look over all I had written during the last several years. Praise and anguish equally shared the pages of my private musings. But as I skimmed each page, one phrase continued to jump out at me. I noticed that every time I addressed the Savior, I wrote, "my Jesus." Over and over, throughout the pages that recorded both heartbreak and breakthrough, I referred to Jesus as *mine.*

When did I start calling Him "my Jesus"? I wondered.

I flipped to entries I had written before the night Jacob had died in the crash but didn't find that phrase on a single page. I only started calling the Lord "my Jesus" *after* losing my brother.

Why, Lord? Why is it that I've only referred to You as my *Jesus over the past three years?* I sat waiting to hear His response.

It's because it's the truth, I heard Him whisper to my heart. *I am yours and you are Mine, Anne. We have a personal relationship.*

I could hardly breathe. The full impact of His words caused me to double over, and my worship came out in tears of gratitude. I, a sinful human, was washed clean and shared an intimate relationship with the almighty God. That had been true since I first accepted Him in seventh grade, but suddenly I understood on a much deeper level. Losing Jacob had opened the reality of eternity up to me like I'd never understood it before. Only through my relationship with Jesus would I be able to see Jacob again. Even more incredible than that, God called me His very own. He wanted me. I belonged to Him.

We all long to be wanted, to belong. We ache to be known and delighted in—not despite but because of that knowing. My heart longed for nothing less. My Jesus knew me, and I knew Him. I heard His voice and sensed His presence. Not because of *my* abilities or goodness, but because of *His*. I was truly His, and He was *my Jesus* now more than ever.

When the shelter-in-place orders finally lifted, we packed up and prepared to head back to Lexington. In many ways, I was relieved to be going back to the comfort of my own home. Yet I felt reluctant to drive away from the farm. And the day our car pulled down the drive headed toward Lexington, I looked out the window up to Jacob's gravesite, where I'd met with God. In that place, I had known such sweet moments of His love and guidance. I had seen the beauty He was already creating out of my greatest loss.

I longed to stay there in the comfort of those familiar hills, but I knew it was time to step back into the reality of my new life and calling. That step involved a lot of unknowns, such as when I would release my single and what song it would be. I didn't know how soon I could return to songwriting or how the pandemic would affect the music industry. I also didn't know how my label would respond to the sound I'd decided upon.

As I gazed out the back window at the farm becoming more and more distant, I reminded myself how much God had already done. I was amazed to think of all He had accomplished in me in a short six weeks. I turned my eyes back to the road before me, took a deep breath, and knew I could trust Him with whatever came next.

A Note from Anne

Leaving a place of comfort and stepping into the unknown is hard. I imagine you've probably had to do that in some form or other. We all have to leave the familiar and forge ahead at times—especially as Christians. A life of faith involves risk. How could it be genuine faith if there were no risk—nothing we had to step out and believe God for?

Leaving the comfort of Wilson Farm during a pandemic and stepping further into the unknown of the music industry was not easy. But it was on the other side of the fear and risk that I met my destiny—the plans God had for me. I have realized that when I stay where I am comfortable, I miss so much. God doesn't call us to a life of comfort; that comes after this life. He calls us to a life of following Him over high mountains and through deep valleys. Not that we don't find comfort in this life—we absolutely do! But we are meant to find it first in God, not in our circumstances. Today, I encourage you to take some steps out of your comfort zone and into what God has planned for you. Know that He, the God of all comfort, goes with you. And He is worthy of any risk or sacrifice.

> All praise to God, the Father of our Lord Jesus Christ. God is our merciful Father and the source of all comfort.
>
> 2 Corinthians 1:3 NLT

TEN

The Release

On September 17, 2020, I walked into Jeff Pardo's home recording studio with butterflies in my stomach. I had returned to writing trips in Nashville a few months earlier, but that day I would be writing with the award-winning Christian singer-songwriter Matthew West, and I was a little starstruck. I had written with Matthew once before during a previous trip, but I still felt nervous being around someone "famous."

Jeff and Matthew greeted me as I walked into the studio. I had barely set down my purse and jacket when Matthew spoke. "Anne, I have this song title idea that I want to tell you about. It's been in my mind all morning."

I sat down and nervously brushed my hair behind my ear. "Sure," I said. "What's the concept?"

"It's a song about having a personal relationship with Jesus," he began, "about belonging to Him and Him belonging to you."

I felt the hair on the back of my neck stand up, but I waited for his next words.

"The title is 'My Jesus,'" he said.

I was silent for a moment, processing what I had just heard. *My Jesus.* I knew he had no way of knowing what those words meant to me—how I had written them in my journal so many times since Jacob died.

"I can't believe you just said that," I said. I started to tell Mathew and Jeff about my six weeks on the farm and what Jesus had done in my heart. I described to them the morning I had met with Jesus at my brother's grave—how I had discovered in my journal that I had begun calling Him "my Jesus" after losing Jacob. And then I shared with them the words Jesus spoke to me—that I was His and He was mine.

That morning on the farm, I had added the title "My Jesus" to my list of song ideas. By the time I had finished sharing that story, I felt complete peace. All nervousness was gone, and I knew the song we'd write that day would be a special one.

As I finished speaking, Matthew and Jeff exchanged a glance. "That's amazing!" Jeff exclaimed. Everyone in the room knew God was up to something.

"Let's get to work," Matthew said.

We began writing with a weighty sense of God's providential hand. I felt His presence as we penned the words and as we developed the melody to the song "My Jesus." As we wrote, we kept in mind my country worship style. Initially, I was concerned about how my label and management might react to the style I'd settled on at the farm, but there was no need for worry. Everyone loved the idea God had given me, saying it was unique and just right for me.

By the end of the writing day with Matthew and Jeff, "My Jesus" was complete and we had a recording ready to submit. We all agreed that this song was meant to be and would surely have a special purpose in the kingdom of God. I didn't suspect it would be my first single, but I knew we had written something important.

Writing sessions usually end at 3:00 p.m., after a day of brainstorming lyrics and melodies. I come in with a song concept, and we all work together to make it a reality. It's common to end a working day with a rough recording of the song called a "worktape." That day, when 3:00 rolled around, instead of calling it a day, Matthew asked Jeff and me to listen to one more thing.

"I can't get this other melody out of my head," he said. "I know we're at the end of the workday, but I need to get this new melody out because I can't stop thinking about it. Maybe there's another song here."

We agreed, and he sang us a melody, using random "da, da, da" sounds. Even without words, Jeff and I were blown away by the haunting tune Matthew sang. I looked over at Jeff just as he turned to me, and I saw that his eyes held the same look as mine—*wow.* A chill ran up my spine.

The three of us decided it was worth working later than planned to develop Matthew's melody into the start of a new song. Matthew knew enough of my story to quickly put words to the first two lines of what is now "No Place Like Home." The rest of the song flowed out of us with little effort but great emotion.

The song was about my Friday drives to the farm with Jacob and how I longed for the day we would be together again in our heavenly home.

Matthew pulled out his guitar, and we sang together to make a worktape recording of the song. After a total of thirty minutes and many tears, we had a second song that day.

After saying our goodbyes, I walked out of Jeff's home and climbed into my car. I had a lot on my mind and even more welling up in my heart. I couldn't believe Matthew and I had both conceived the same song title—"My Jesus"—one that was so dear to my heart and my own personal journey. That could only be God.

I put my car in drive and slowly pulled out of his driveway, heading back to the apartment my parents and I had been renting in Nashville. My writing trips had become so frequent that we needed a place to stay in when we were in town. I wouldn't move into that little apartment full-time until the following year.

As I drove home, the excitement of writing "My Jesus" quickly slipped into all the heavy emotions stirred up while writing "No Place Like Home." The song described some of my favorite memories with my brother and the struggle to live without him. Each line we had written pulled up beautiful yet painful images of my childhood with Jacob.

I tried to hold back the tears, but I couldn't. I ached for Jacob. There was no one around to see, so I let the tears come. I'd just been singing a beautifully sad melody about climbing up High Point Mountain with Jacob, and my heart felt like it would burst from remembrance and longing. If only I could bring him back for another climb up that mountain.

When I arrived back at my little apartment, my parents were out, so I curled up by myself on the tan couch and contemplated the mixed emotions heavy on my chest. Normally I would put those feelings aside and distract myself with work, but that day I didn't. I was grateful for God's inspiration to write two songs, but I was also sad and hurting—maybe even a little angry. I didn't want to have this story to tell. That's the cost of writing from the deep places. You hold extreme joy and crushing pain in your heart at the same time. I found myself praying the songs would bring hope to others who were hurting and offer them a real relationship with Jesus.

I texted a clip of "My Jesus" to Jason so he could hear it, and a few minutes later, my phone rang.

"Anne," he said, "this song is incredible! This might be the one—I think this is your single."

I shared his excitement over the song, but I wasn't yet convinced "My Jesus" was *the* song. It took me three months to fully see what others immediately saw in that song. During those months I continued to write, but no other songs emerged that felt as special as "My Jesus" and "No Place Like Home." Eventually, I realized "My Jesus" had the potential to touch the most people and meet them wherever they were. In December, a year after signing with Capitol, I followed the advice of those working with me in the industry and decided on "My Jesus" as my very first single.

That January, I began the process of recording the song. Producing one single takes many days in studio as the musicians and vocalists record the song in layers. Then the recording goes through an extensive mixing and editing process.

On the day I was scheduled to record my vocals for the song, I woke up feeling ill, but I decided I could power through the day. I said goodbye to my mom, who was at the apartment with me, and headed to the studio. Throughout the entire day, I felt nauseated and dizzy. I made it through recording, but just barely. On the drive home, I pulled into a grocery store parking lot and ran into the store's bathroom to be sick. I was so repeatedly and violently ill that I called my mom for help. She was back at the apartment and told me to stay put—she was coming to get me.

Back at home, I continued to vomit until I was completely dehydrated, with nothing left to come out of me. Finally, around 9:00 that night, Mom decided I needed medical attention and took me to the nearest urgent care clinic. I sat out in the car in the parking lot while she went inside to register.

"Anne, if you need me for anything, just honk the horn, and I'll come right out." She could tell by my shaking body and pale face that this was not an ordinary stomach bug. I nodded and closed my eyes.

A few minutes later, I opened the door to be sick again and then lay back in my seat, numb and shaking. I felt like my body was shutting down, and I feared I was dying. I reached my hand over and, with what strength I had left, laid on the horn. Mom came running out and opened the car door.

"Mom," I said, "I feel like I'm dying." She took one look at my barely open eyes and trembling body and knew I was telling the truth.

"We're going to the hospital!" she said. She buckled in and called my dad. "Kent, honey, listen. Anne is so sick that I'm taking her to the hospital. It's serious. I need you to pray for us right now."

Mom hung up, put the car in reverse, and headed for the hospital. I barely remember the drive there or getting checked in. They admitted me right away and proceeded to hook me up to an IV and run multiple tests. The results of the MRI and blood work revealed that I had a severe intestinal infection. They immediately began to administer an antibiotic.

"Ma'am," the doctor said in a serious tone. "Your daughter could have died if you hadn't brought her in." He explained that because of the infection, nothing could pass through my intestinal tract, which was why I couldn't hold anything down.

With an IV line replenishing my fluids and providing medicine to treat the infection, I began to feel better quickly. What a relief to be able to lie still with no vomiting or shaking. I turned to look at my mom and saw relief in her face as well.

"Mom, God must be doing something big with this song," I said weakly. "The devil is trying so hard to stop it. I think he tried to kill me tonight."

"Oh, Anne, I think you're right!" she said. I saw tears in her eyes. "But thank God He protected you. He is definitely going to do something amazing." I realized then how scary the whole ordeal must have been for her, fearing she might lose a second child. Thankfully, God did not let that happen. I recovered quickly and was able to leave the hospital the next day.

Opening My Heart

With the upcoming release of "My Jesus," my management and I planned to simultaneously release a music video of the song. The goal of the video was to capture the heart of our tragedy and how we turned to Jesus in the middle of our pain. In March, we met with potential actors who might portray us in the video. It was not hard to sense which people would best represent us in both looks and spirit. The little girl we chose to play me was so precious—just perfect for the heart of this video.

We filmed the scenes at a church first but soon moved on to a doctor's office to film. My family and I sat behind the scenes and watched the story unfold as they were taping. Even though our story did not actually involve getting the news of Jacob's death at a hospital, the video captured the extreme pain of the moment we heard it. Watching the filming scraped open every wound in me from the trauma of that day.

I lowered my head and wept. Something inside me was breaking. It wasn't my heart. That had already happened many times over. This time it was my controlled exterior. As the wounds were reopened, I realized just how much I had been pushing down my pain. In trying to be strong for so long, I realized that I had not fully accepted it. In a moment, I surveyed my life and saw that I'd been stuck at various levels of denial and depression for more than three years, while pretending to be okay.

I didn't understand how I had let that happen. I knew the relief I felt at Jacob's graveside, when I couldn't distract myself from the reality that he was gone. While the past few years had been a whirlwind of amazing experiences and even spiritual growth, the crazy events in my life had served as distractions, keeping me from dealing with my grief. I pretended I was the strong one when beneath the surface I was barely keeping it together. I was angry with myself that I'd been doing this for so long, and I was exhausted from the effort of keeping up a facade for everyone around me.

The pain I felt that day was so deep down inside me, I knew I would need help to process it. I needed someone to guide me through grieving and accepting my brother's death. As I sat watching the actors portray the day my brother died, I determined I would make time for my own healing and find a counselor to walk with me through the process.

I looked over at my dad and mom and then at my sister. They, too, were quietly crying. I knew each of them had accepted Jacob's passing more than I had. None of us would ever be "over it," but they were further along in the grieving process than I was. On some level, I felt like I was stuck in a pit with no motivation or passion for life. And I didn't think I could get out on my own. I needed someone to help me process through the grief. It was time for me to get unstuck.

At the end of the day, when we climbed into our car, all of us were emotionally spent.

"Wow," I said, shutting my door. Silence. None of us had words for what we'd just experienced. Even if we had, no one had the energy to speak them out loud. I exhaled slowly as Daddy drove off. Back at the apartment, I thought about how good the raw video footage had looked. In a single day, the vision we had for the "My Jesus" video had come to life before our eyes. It was incredible, and I believed God would use the video in a massive way. *Maybe He'll even save a life through it,* I thought. I wasn't thinking about views or comments; I was thinking about salvations and stories.

The song and music video of "My Jesus" would be released at midnight on April 16, 2021. In the hours leading up it, I was alone in my apartment in Nashville.

With midnight on the East Coast approaching, I knelt on the cowhide rug in my living room and surrendered to God, much like I had done back in the seventh grade when I chose Him for the first time. This time, in the dim lamplight of my own place, I was releasing my single and everything that came after into His hands. I laid before Him my concerns about how people might react to my song and what the next steps of my musical journey would look like. I gave up my desire to know every step of the plan and consecrated my future to God. Jacob was always trying to help me loosen the reins on my need for a plan. I may not have learned that lesson from him, but that night in my apartment, I took a big step forward in the process.

"My Jesus, I surrender to You," I prayed. "I give You today and all the days that follow. And I'm asking You with everything in me to use this song to impact people for the gospel. Even if You use this song or video to save just one life, that's all that matters to me. I release the song to You, God, to do with it what You want. I trust You."

Thirty minutes after I released the song into God's hands, it was released onto music platforms across the nation.

The next evening my family and I gathered to celebrate the

release of my single with Jason, the team from Capitol Music, and folks from the booking agency. Cast and crew from the music video also joined us for a casual dinner and outdoor viewing of the finished video. It felt surreal to be celebrating the release of a song. I was only nineteen, but I felt as though I'd lived an entire lifetime since Jacob left us.

A day after the release party, Jason FaceTimed me at 10:35 p.m. with some news. "Anne," he said, "'My Jesus' is number one on the iTunes Christian Chart!"

"Are you serious?!" I could not believe what I was hearing and began to cry.

"This song is skyrocketing in a way rarely seen for a debut artist," Jason said. God was already doing more than I had ever expected, and He was doing it in record time.

Five days after the release of the song, I heard it on the radio, as the folks at WBGL in Champaign, Illinois, played it for the very first time over the airwaves. I did several interviews with the people at WBGL in the following days and developed a sweet friendship with them. After hearing "My Jesus" on the radio, I wrote on my Instagram page, "Am I in a dream or what?" That is exactly how it felt—like I was living a dream too good for words. I could not stop smiling that day.

A Sudden Shift

And then my life changed dramatically overnight. Within a month of releasing "My Jesus," almost every hour of every day for the rest of my year was booked solid with writing, touring, and recording. I barely had time to catch my breath before I headed out to play the summer music festival circuit. I officially became a "road dog," traveling by car and plane constantly, getting little to no sleep, and finding rest any place I could. In truth, it began the hardest season of my life, outside of losing Jacob.

After "My Jesus" released, I moved to my Nashville apartment. I had to be in Nashville all the time, so living in Lexington was impossible. I was suddenly pulled away from the only home I'd ever known. I loved what I was doing and where I lived, but I was also lonely. I missed my family, my friends, my mentor Erica, and my community back in Lexington.

The counseling I'd promised myself during the making of the music video started in June, and the timing could not have been better. Before we even began to work on processing Jacob's death, I needed help adjusting to my new life. No one had expected "My Jesus" to blow up the way it did. We were unprepared. My parents had to finish up their own obligations in Lexington before they could be with me as much as they wanted. My life was suddenly very hectic, and I was dealing with the natural change in friendships from moving away.

Not only was I in a different state from everyone I loved, I was also living a completely different lifestyle than they were. I wasn't attending college classes or hanging out with friends on the weekend like other nineteen-year-olds. I was traveling the country, giving concerts, and telling my story to thousands of strangers. As much as I loved telling people about what Jesus had done in my life, it also made it hard to connect with my childhood friends because we were living such different lives.

In those lonely months, I cherished the moments I had with God. I rarely had free time, but when I did, I liked to shut down my technology and escape from the demands of the music world for a little while. I could curl up with my Bible and feel "normal" again, being reminded that in a changing world, my God was unchanging.

Over the course of the summer, I continued to go to counseling as often as I could, fitting it in around my crazy travel schedule. My parents and I were often driving late into the night or taking cross-country flights. Excitement for these new opportunities was high, but my energy and emotional reserves were very low.

The round of summer festivals would wrap up in late August. On August 21, Jacob's birthday, I was scheduled to play at a large festival in Gothenburg, Nebraska. His birthday and the anniversary of his death are hard days for me, and I had always set those days aside for private grieving. I had told my schedulers about the dates, but they had still tentatively booked me to play the festival. A week before Jacob's birthday, I was wrestling with whether I had the emotional strength to do the show.

One afternoon, as we drove to yet another venue, I asked Daddy for his thoughts.

"Anne, I can't tell you what to do," he said. "Ask the Lord for guidance and do what you feel He's asking you to. You might need the time alone, or God might have something different in mind." Daddy paused then spoke again. "I've been thinking—wouldn't it be amazing if 'My Jesus' hit number one on the radio charts near Jacob's birthday? What a birthday gift."

"That would be incredible," I agreed. But I suspected we weren't anywhere near that happening.

I continued to pray about the Gothenburg show and finally decided to do it. I'd been feeling a persistent sense that I should. I was reluctant to commit because I didn't know how the day would affect me. But a desire to obey God's leading won out.

That evening in Nebraska was beautiful—blue skies with a few wispy clouds and a slight breeze to cool us. I stood on the stage in the middle of my set, thousands of people in front of me, and I knew why I was there. This was the fruition of what I most wanted to do since losing Jacob—tell people about my Jesus while they still had time to choose Him. And at that moment onstage, I had the opportunity to do so before thousands of people.

I'm so sorry that I was reluctant to do this show, Father God, I silently prayed. *Why would I not want to be up here doing this—seeing You fulfill the dreams You've put in my heart? Of all days, I should most want to share Jesus with others on Jacob's birthday. Thank You for giving me this chance, God.*

I returned home to Lexington very late the next night. When I crawled out of bed in the morning, still exhausted and low on sleep, I saw a message from Jason: "Let's have a video call as soon as possible. It's urgent."

I pulled myself together quickly and called him from my room. Jason and his wife, Heather, were on the screen together.

"Anne! Your song just went number one on the Christian radio charts!"

I called my parents into the room, and the three of us stood hugging each other and crying. Could God be *this* good? Did He really hear what Daddy had said and make it happen? I had just played the show on Jacob's birthday two nights earlier, and now "My Jesus" was number one, while it was still his birthday weekend. The timing was too close to be a coincidence. I knew it was a gift from God, and I knew exactly where I wanted to go to commemorate it.

We drove out to Wilson Farm late in the afternoon and walked up the gravel lane to Jacob's grave. If I had not been out on the road doing shows, I would have been there on his birthday, like I had been every August 21 since he died. Now I wanted to share with Jacob all that had happened at the concert and that morning with my song. I knew he wasn't really in the grave to hear me, but somehow it helped me to process it out loud, there where he was buried.

While my family stood huddled together a short distance away, I took a seat near his gravestone and whispered, "Jacob, you won't believe what God just did—well, no, you probably will. You probably already know all about it. But Jacob, just like Daddy imagined, 'My Jesus' became a number one song on your birthday weekend." My voice broke a little, and I looked up to the hill where we had spent so many hours laughing and shooting together. I let out a deep breath. "I just can't believe what God has done—how good He is. He let me tell thousands of people about Him on your birthday, Jacob. Isn't that the best birthday gift? Jacob . . . I miss you so much I can't stand it. Honestly, I'd trade it all in a heartbeat to have you back with me." I had to pause to catch my breath. I reached down and pressed my hand to the cool grass to ground myself back in the moment.

"But that's not how this works, is it?" A tear slid down my cheek. "I know it's not. And I know God is doing something incredible for His kingdom. He's making something beautiful from the wreckage of our lives. And . . . I just wanted to tell you about it. I love you, Jacob."

That night, I stood with my sister and my parents at Jacob's grave and watched one of the most magnificent sunsets I've ever seen. Giant billowing clouds were lit up by the golden rays of light shooting out from behind the hills and across the sky. It was a gift from our good Father. There, in the very place that represented our deep grief, was God's amazing beauty. And I knew He wasn't finished yet; He was just getting started. The breathtaking sunset was a reminder of all He had done for us and how He had brought us through our tragedy. And it was a promise that He would never leave us.

I needed that reminder badly. My heart was still in a precarious place. I was continuing to adjust to such a dramatic life change as I dove deeper into my healing through counseling journey. I wasn't naive enough to expect life to get easier right away, but I was more assured than ever that I wouldn't face a minute of it alone.

A Note from Anne

For months following Jacob's death, I found ways to repress my grief so I wouldn't be a burden to anyone. I felt stuck, like I couldn't fully heal. If you find yourself in the same place, I encourage you to reach out for help. You don't have to do this alone. Getting help is not only okay; it's a wise thing to do. We seek help from professionals in almost every other area of life: auto repair, construction, plumbing, and health care. There is no shame in finding a professional to help walk you through difficult things in your life. Counseling is simply a scheduled time to look inward with trained professional guidance.

I am so grateful for the Christ-centered counseling I have received and continue to receive. It's been a literal Godsend. I only wish I could have started it sooner! Before I took this step, God used His Word to counsel me, and I spent many hours reading Scripture. He also brought mature Christians into my life to offer me guidance and encouragement. In His perfect timing, He opened the doors for me to seek out a professional counselor. If you need help but feel you don't have access, ask God for what you need and then reach out to your local church. Many congregations offer free counseling services and can help you know where to start. God will be faithful to provide all that you need.

> My God shall supply all your need according to His riches in glory by Christ Jesus.
>
> PHILIPPIANS 4:19 NKJV

ELEVEN

Seasons of Hope

I SAT IN ONE OF MY FAVORITE LITTLE COFFEE SHOPS IN Nashville with a steaming almond milk latte in my hands. I had a short break between a management meeting and vocal lessons, and I needed a few minutes to recenter. My manager and I were in the process of finding an artist I could open for on my first official tour in the fall of 2021. I knew this decision would have a profound influence on my professional growth and who I would become as an artist. The summer festivals I'd played had given me valuable stage experience, but this would be my first experience with an actual tour—three months on the road with the same group of people singing the same songs. I knew I wanted to start with an artist who would model for me what a God-centered tour looks like.

My manager, Jason, had his eye on Big Daddy Weave, a well-known Christian band led by front man Mike Weaver. Jason told me about the integrity of the group and their obvious heart for ministry. Everyone I'd spoken to had echoed Jason's thoughts—if I wanted to learn how to tour while keeping God as my central focus, Big Daddy Weave could show me how. I had asked my circle in Nashville to pray I would get an offer to open for them. But, as the situation was rolling around in my thoughts there in the coffee shop, I called my mom to ask her to pray as well.

After I told her about Big Daddy Weave and their reputation, Mom said, "They sound like they might be the right fit for you, honey. Hold on a sec while I pull them up on YouTube." I waited while Mom played a video from one of their concerts.

"Oh, Anne, this looks perfect," she said, the music still playing in the background. "Daddy and I will be praying constantly about this for you. Whether it's Big Daddy Weave or someone else, that's the kind of concert you want to be a part of!"

The excitement in my mom's voice mirrored the growing anticipation in my heart. My greatest desire in going on tour was to share with others what Jesus had done in my life. I knew I needed to learn from people in the industry who had been consistently and successfully doing just that. After I ended the call with my mom, I prayed again that God would provide the perfect first tour for me. And I added that I wouldn't mind if it were Big Daddy Weave.

A few weeks later, while I was home in Lexington, my parents joined me in the living room for an important call from Jason. We squeezed together on the couch, and I put my phone on speaker.

"Guys, you better be sitting down for this. I have some good news," Jason said. "Anne, I just met with Mike Weaver, and Big Daddy Weave made you an offer to open for them on tour this fall! It's *exactly* what we prayed for."

"That's incredible!" I cried, jumping up from my seat and almost dropping the phone. "I can hardly believe it! God answered so quickly!"

We immediately accepted the offer. I was grateful a group the caliber of Big Daddy Weave was willing to take a chance on me, a brand-new artist. The tour would be called All Things New, which also seemed tailor-made for me.

I joined the band for a week of rehearsals just before our opening show on September 22. Mike had chosen a collaborative format for the concert. I would open the shows with several of my songs. Then Big Daddy Weave would join me onstage to sing "My Jesus" together. After that, I'd leave the stage until the end—when I joined them again for four final songs.

I didn't get a chance to read through those songs until the first day of rehearsals. As I read the lyrics of "All Things New," I realized that Mike and the guys of Big Daddy Weave had intentionally chosen me to sing this song with them. They knew my story, and it was no coincidence that they had asked me to sing about God making something beautiful out of deep pain and a broken heart. I was blown away by their kindness and the obvious leading of the Holy Spirit in including me.

Each night of the tour, Mike welcomed me back onstage to sing the second verse of that song. Each time I sang the song with them was a powerful moment and a new chance to surrender myself to God. White lights filled the stage, illuminating the crowd of worshipers before us. They sang with hands raised to the One who makes all things new. As I sang, every single word rang true. God was in the process of making all things new in my life. Being on the All Things New tour with Big Daddy Weave and singing that song wasn't happenstance. God orchestrated it all because He knew exactly what I needed.

During the three months we were on the road, we traveled to twenty-five cities. I learned valuable lessons from Big Daddy Weave about performing, but I learned more about loving people. I saw the band members honor God in their daily decisions and in how they used their time. Each night before the concert, we held a Q and A for certain ticketholders. I was impressed by how Mike and the guys took their time with the questions and tried to make a personal connection with each person. They would even stop to pray if someone expressed a need. Even in the midst of a hectic tour schedule, they loved people well.

Whether onstage or enjoying a late-night meal at Waffle House, they exhibited the kingdom of God in the way they spoke from stage or the kind words they spoke to the server. They were thoughtful and considerate of me and full of stories that kept me laughing. I felt like I had a whole group of big brothers who knew exactly what it was like living the tour life. My parents joined me on tour every night possible, and the guys of Big Daddy Weave welcomed them in like family, showing them great honor.

During one of our final shows, in Quincy, Illinois, I finally had a chance to watch the entire show from start to finish. Typically I would write emails or attend to work during that time, so I had never watched the entire concert. That night, I took a break from my work and stood backstage with my parents to watch every bit of the show. What I witnessed left me in awe. This was not a performance. This was a ministry.

When Mike invited people to come down to the altar if they wanted a touch from Jesus, I began to weep uncontrollably. Men, women, and even children flocked to the front of the auditorium. Many dropped to their knees and put their faces to the ground as they cried out to Jesus for salvation and help.

This is it, I thought. *This is exactly what I want my future touring to be like. I want people to experience Jesus like this.* Nothing about that night was about Big Daddy Weave—it was all about Jesus. And I knew God was calling me to proclaim Him in the same way.

Christmas Preparations

The All Things New tour ended November 14, and I immediately began rehearsals for my Christmas tour with Zach Williams. That opportunity was literally a dream come true for me. The previous spring, my booking agency had asked me: If I could pick anyone, who would I most want to tour with? I quickly said Zach Williams, one of my favorite Christian artists. I had loved his sound since 2016 when he released his hit single "Chain Breaker."

A month after that conversation, I received an offer to open for Zach on his Christmas tour, called I Don't Want Christmas to End. That led me to immediately develop ideas for Christmas songs. That August I cowrote a song with Jeff Pardo and Matthew

West called "I Still Believe in Christmas." I wanted to write an honest Christmas song for the people who struggle with grief and depression during the holiday season. I knew what it felt like to wish that Christmas would just hurry on past because the season felt too painful. Writing that song was a sweet way for me to express the sadness of celebrating the season without Jacob and share the goodness of God in sending His Son.

When I joined Zach on his Christmas tour, I was able to share the good news of Jesus through "I Still Believe in Christmas." I also had the privilege of sharing the stage with Zach to sing "There Was Jesus," his number one song with Dolly Parton. Night after night, I felt incredibly honored to sing the part originated by Dolly Parton. I could hardly believe all that my Jesus had made possible for me.

Journey into Wholeness

While touring with Big Daddy Weave and Zach Williams, I looked forward to several days at home in Nashville in between legs of the tour. Those days at home allowed me to continue my counseling journey. But I had to fight for it. Many other responsibilities laid claim to my time, so I had to be tenacious about setting aside time for my own healing.

That fall I entered into the deep work of accepting and processing Jacob's death. My counselor helped me realize it was okay not to be okay, even out on tour. She encouraged me not to push the pain down when it came, but instead give myself permission to be sad—even all day long, if that's what I was feeling. I started practicing emotional honesty with myself and those around me. When a longing for Jacob was triggered, I no longer distracted myself from the pain. I let myself sit in it. I let myself feel it.

My counselor explained to me the stages of the grief cycle—denial, anger, bargaining, depression, acceptance. For the first time, I understood I could and should be honest about my anger. Up to that point, I had not allowed myself to acknowledge, let alone feel, my anger. My counselor explained that repressed anger leads to depression. (No wonder I'd been stuck in depression and denial!) So I began to be honest with myself about my feelings. I felt angry that Jacob was gone. I had to tell myself over and over that it was okay to be angry. Even God gets angry. I acknowledged that it made me mad that death even exists. Death had robbed me of my brother. Slowly, I was stepping out of denial and into anger.

I am still working my way through this process. Even now, I experience times of depression and times of acceptance. Sometimes I try to bargain with God, but I am learning to surrender and rest. This has always come easily to me at Jacob's grave, but I'm learning to surrender the pain wherever I am. All through the fluctuating process, I've learned I can be honest about my emotions without letting them control me. It is critical that I trust God, not my emotions, to lead me, but I must also honor what I am feeling. For so long, I had been scared to let my emotions out for fear they would destroy me or hurt others. I trusted God in other areas of my life, and I could trust Him with my painful emotions.

Counseling helped me see that this healing journey will never be over. While I have come to a place of greater wholeness through it, I will never fully recover from losing Jacob, and I don't want to. I don't want to be "over it." That would dishonor his memory. My goal is to be an emotionally healthy adult who can step into every opportunity God has for me.

Hebrews 4:11 says we must strive to enter into the rest of God and not succumb to unbelief. I've never found that to be truer than in my healing journey. I must fight to enter that restful place of surrender, clawing my way past temptations to shut down, deny, or numb my pain. I check in with myself every day to make sure I'm not bottling up difficult emotions. If I am, I walk through those feelings and surrender them to God. If I go a few days without doing a self check-in, I can feel it. The internal pressure builds, and my emotions start to plummet. Then I know it's time to get honest again with myself and with Jesus. It's a daily battle.

Sometimes I will stare at pictures of Jacob or bury my face in one of his flannel shirts and let myself remember. The tears fall, and I sink into the deep ache of missing him and longing to see him again. Instead of putting a Band-Aid on it, I let the wound breathe. And then I eventually dry my tears and move forward with the knowledge that this pain will not overcome me. I have finally faced the reality that my brother is gone, and it did not destroy me. With each passing day, my Jesus has walked me into a deeper acceptance of that loss and all it means for me. I trust Him with all the hard days still to come, because I know He'll be there too.

Surprising Gifts

That Christmas was the first since losing Jacob that I didn't feel completely depressed the entire season. My family and I put up a few decorations. We also decided to exchange gifts, something we had not formally done since Jacob's death. It felt good to enjoy a bit of the season and realize my healing was progressing.

The Monday before Christmas, I was at my Nashville apartment with Daddy when I received a text from my manager that "I Still Believe in Christmas" had just hit number one on Billboard's Christian Airplay chart. In a single week, the song had jumped from number nine to number one—the biggest jump to number one for a female Christian artist the chart's editor had ever seen.

Ever since I'd written that song, I had felt nervous about it. I wondered if it was good enough to release. Though Jeff and Matthew assured me the song would resonate, I worried it was too sad for a Christmas song. Many Christmas songs released in the Christian market are bright and happy, and for good reason. We have much to celebrate in Jesus' coming to earth to be our Savior and to bring His joy. But there are many who feel devastated at Christmastime, like my family and me, who, that first Christmas without Jacob, tried to escape the pain of it by distracting ourselves at Biltmore. I know celebrating the season can be hard for those dealing with pain in their lives, such as a recent divorce, the death of a loved one, an illness, or financial hardship. I wrote the song for those people. Still, I had no idea how others might receive it or if they'd even like it.

When I learned that "I Still Believe in Christmas" had hit

number one, I started crying. I whispered to Jesus, "You've done it again. I've been doubting that song for months, but You did it. You knew I needed that song, and You knew the world needed that song. Thank You, God."

I felt the gentle nudge of His Spirit reminding me that He was using my desire to write honest songs for hurting people and doing something only He could do. I may have doubted, but this was His plan all along. When I shared the news with Daddy, his eyes welled up.

"I'm so proud of you, Anne," he said, embracing me. "Look what God is doing. He is so proud of you. Jacob is so proud of you."

Daddy is a man of few words, but when he speaks, we listen because we know he means what he says. His words that day went straight to my heart.

A day later, Daddy and I headed home to Kentucky to spend our fifth Christmas without Jacob. I discovered I could face it with less fear and depression than in previous years, because I was thinking about how God was using my song to provide hope and comfort to many people. Because of it, I felt a renewed sense of purpose that Christmas season. My family felt it too.

Two days before Christmas, Liz and I spent a lazy evening in the living room. After looking down at her phone, she suddenly jerked her head up and told me I needed to go to the front door.

"Why?" I asked, not wanting to move from my comfortable spot on the couch. "Can you go?"

"No," Liz said, a mischievous glint in her eye. "Emma and Sarah just dropped off a present for you. You better go see what it is."

I pulled myself up off the couch and padded to the front door. I opened it and looked out. No one was there. I was about to shut the door when I glanced down and saw a cardboard box on the front step. All I could see in the box was a little blanket. When I stepped closer, I saw a tiny brown head pop up from within the blanket, and the cutest blue eyes stared back at me. *A puppy!* But not just any puppy—a Boykin spaniel, just like Sallie. Liz had bought me a Boykin spaniel puppy for Christmas.

I bent over and scooped the little ball of brown fluff into my arms. As I held him, I cried into his soft brown fur, thinking of Jacob. The new life of that little puppy comforted me and filled me with hope. I scratched his little curly head and spoke sweet words to my puppy. I felt like a kid again. We had lost Sallie six months earlier, marking the first time in sixteen years that our family was without a pet. In losing Jacob and then Sallie, I felt like a part of my childhood had died. Standing there holding that new puppy felt so right—like a bit of my youth had been restored.

"What should we call him?" I asked my sister.

"I already know his name," Liz said. "Anne, last week I dreamed of Jacob again. It felt so real, like I was speaking right to him. At the end of the dream, Jacob told me to name your puppy Hank Williams."

I brushed back tears. "Hello, Hank," I said, stroking his little nose. I looked up at my sister. "He's perfect, Liz. And every time I say his name, I'll think of Jacob. I don't know how to thank you. This is the sweetest thing ever."

Even though Hank is not Jacob's dog, he's connected to Jacob because of Liz's dream. He's a new little life, and receiving him ushered in a new season of hope for me. That Christmas wasn't perfect, but it was a little easier. I had an adorable puppy to love on and a heart that was healing. I could see how God was already using my suffering and the songs I was writing to bring hope to thousands of hurting people.

One of my favorite verses is Romans 5:3–5, which says we should rejoice in our sufferings because they lead to perseverance, which leads to character, which leads to hope. And hope does not disappoint. If I had not persevered through suffering, allowing God to build my character and lead me into hope, I would never have understood this was possible. How can suffering actually *result* in hope? In surrendering my deepest pain to Him, I watched my Jesus bring something truly miraculous out of it. My hope isn't that I won't face suffering again. It's a hope that no matter what I face, God will be there with me in it, working it for my good.

A Hopeful Heart

On a recent trip through Florida on tour, I escaped to a nearby beach to recharge and enjoy the beauty of God's creation. As I walked barefoot through the sand, my mind wandered back to the evening Jacob had taken me on that bike ride to watch the sunset together. Neither of us knew it would be the last ride we would share. I relived every moment of that evening in my mind, but what I really longed for was to relive it in person.

As I allowed myself to feel the ache of remembering, I thought of something significant that happened three years after Jacob had died and only a couple months before writing "My Jesus." Though we had continued to take a summer vacation in Florida after we lost Jacob, our first two summers back, we couldn't bring ourselves to stay in the same beach house. We rented a house in a neighboring beach town instead. Each year, I had tried driving around the area where we used to stay to find Jacob's sunset beach. But I never found it.

The third summer we returned, as the COVID-19 lockdowns were beginning to lift, we settled into the same small white beach house we'd rented with Jacob. That year, I was determined I would find our beach and walk again where Jacob and I had walked. I longed to relive one of our last and sweetest memories together.

Though I searched every day, I could not find the beach. I tried retracing the route we had taken on our bikes, but my memory failed me. That day three years earlier, I had just been following Jacob and enjoying his company. As the last day of our vacation dawned, I was feeling extremely discouraged.

"I guess I'm just not going to find our special sunset place," I told my mom, tears of frustration filling my eyes.

"I'm so sorry, Anne." Mom gently brushed her hand against my cheek. "Do you think maybe God doesn't want us to find it?"

"You may be right." I sighed with resignation. "Maybe He doesn't. That's okay." But my shoulders slumped as I turned to walk away.

"Honey," Mom said. "What if we rent paddleboards today, like we did with Jacob on that last trip?"

I turned back to her, a smile lighting my face. "That would be perfect, Mom. Thank you!" I knew this was a financial sacrifice for us, and she was doing it to cheer me up. I immediately began researching paddleboard rentals and making a plan.

I scheduled the boards to arrive at one o'clock that afternoon. But later that morning I received a call from the paddleboard company, telling me the waves were too high and we wouldn't be able to take the boards out. I called my mom from the beach with the disappointing news.

After explaining the situation, I said, "The paddleboard guy is on his way over to the house to give us a refund. Liz and I will head back to meet you."

"Hold on!" Elizabeth interrupted. "Let me talk to Mom."

I handed her the phone. "Mom, listen," she said. "We can't take that refund. I know firsthand how hard COVID-19 has been on small businesses, and we just can't do that to this guy. He's running his own business here and trying to stay afloat. I feel strongly about this. Don't take the money back."

"Elizabeth, honey, I don't even know what to say," Mom said. "I'm so proud of you. You're right. I'll tell him we don't want a refund."

We arrived back at the rental house just as Mom was telling the gentleman that we did not want our money back. The look on his face showed us how much this gesture meant to him.

"Thank you," he said. "Thank you so much." He paused thoughtfully and then said, "There is one beach that might be calm enough for you to use the paddleboards there today. I would just hate for you not to get any use out of them, especially when you've been so generous."

"That'd be amazing!" I said. "Where is it?"

"Well, it's kind of hard to find," the man continued. "How about I just lead the way, and you can follow me there."

Mom, Liz, and I grabbed our beach bags and piled into our car. We followed the man on a long drive that took many twists and turns. He was right—we never would have found that place on our own.

When we finally stopped, I hopped out of the car first, eager to see if the water were indeed calm enough to take out the paddleboards. But as I neared the edge of the beach, I dropped to my knees.

"Anne?! What's wrong?" my mom called out. She began running toward me with concern.

"Mom," I said. "This is it! This is Jacob's beach. This is where he brought me for our sunset together three years ago." My sobs choked out the rest of my words.

Mom knelt on the sand and wrapped her arms around me. Elizabeth knelt with us, and the three of us leaned our heads together. We sat together on the hot sand for what felt like hours, undone by the goodness of God. I had not even asked God to help me find our sunset beach. I'd just been searching for it on my own. But Jesus knew the desire of my heart. And He planned the whole thing out perfectly, just like Jacob had done three years before. I knew He did it for me.

As I looked out at the tranquil waves years later, the sweet memory of finding Jacob's beach filled me with expectation. Who knew what other surprises God had in store for me? I stood by the water's edge, knowing I needed to leave this place and return to the demanding reality of tour life. But first, I took a moment to thank God for His faithfulness to me. I raised my hands in worship to the One who knows and fulfills the deepest desires of my heart—even dreams I didn't know to hope for.

I looked out to where the ocean meets the sky—a line where the two don't end but stretch on together almost endlessly. It only looks like an ending. That point on the horizon always reminds me of eternity, where Jacob is waiting for me.

I sighed deeply and allowed myself to feel the sadness of being away from him, but even as I wiped my tears, I smiled. I know the day will come, sooner than I can imagine, when I will run into my brother's arms, and it will feel like just moments since we last hugged. But the greatest joy will be when I see the face of the One who walked with me through my deepest pain—the One who wove together all the beautiful moments of my life—and I run into the arms of my Jesus.

EPILOGUE

A Final Note from Anne

Five years have passed since Jacob died, and sometimes it's still hard to believe he's gone. During those years, I have walked through many days when I felt hopeless, yet God has brought me through each one. I often long for Jacob and remember all the beautiful memories we have, the lessons he taught me, and the fifteen years I was blessed to have him as my big brother. I'm grateful I have the enduring hope of seeing him again in heaven. Sometimes it feels like it will be forever until that day comes, when really, forever is what I will get to spend with Jacob.

When I think back to my darkest days of grief and reflect on all God has done since that time, His faithfulness is the consistent thread I see woven through it all. From the very first moment when He asked me to trust Him until now, I see His hand in my life. He has upheld me in my most painful moments and has fulfilled His promise to bring good out of every situation—even losing Jacob.

God has provided exactly what I need at every turn and been my constant help and comfort. He has calmed the fears in my heart with His love and shown me how to find joy even in unimaginable loss. His Word has been "a lamp to my feet" (Psalm 119:105 NKJV), and He has shown me each next step I am to walk. I trust Him for the future, whatever it holds. I'm excited to see what He has in store. The journey into a music career singing His praises has already been more than I could have dreamed, and I know He's not finished. There are good days ahead.

Right now, my days are full of creating music, touring, and telling people about *my Jesus.* That is my greatest joy. I love watching people's faces as they listen to me share about the grace and comfort Jesus offers in suffering and then as they raise their hands to worship Him too. Sometimes I can't believe God chose me for this great honor—offering the hope He's given me to thousands of others. It's incredible. But my greatest hope of all is the forever future I have with Christ. I pray that every day, as I walk with Him and tell the world how good He is, I bring a smile to His face. For I am His, and He is mine. He is my Jesus.

> May our Lord Jesus Christ Himself and God our Father, who has loved us and given us eternal comfort and good hope by grace, comfort and strengthen your hearts in every good work and word.
>
> 2 THESSALONIANS 2:16–17 NASB

Acknowledgments

Thank you to my precious family. My mom, my dad, and my beautiful sister, you all have stuck by me and supported me step-by-step. I love you all deeply.

Marcie Maggart, thank you for writing this book with me. Your excellence in this craft is mind-blowing. I am forever grateful for you and the way you brought this book to life.

Thank you, Story House Collective and Crowd Surf, for helping launch this book in the best way. Your support is everything.

To my precious brother in heaven, you are the reason this book came to be. Thank you for the legacy you left on this earth.

Last—but not least—thank You, my Jesus, for loving me deeply and never leaving my side. You are my greatest love and treasure. This is for You.

About the Author

Anne Wilson grew up in Kentucky with her parents and two siblings, Elizabeth and Jacob. Her family's Christian faith sustained them through the tragic loss of Jacob when he was only twenty-three years old. She is passionate about writing and singing songs that draw others to Jesus. Anne's debut single, "My Jesus," became the #1 Christian song of 2021 and won the Breakout Single of the Year at the 2022 K-LOVE Fan Awards, where Anne also won Female Artist of the Year.

Learn more about Anne and her music and touring schedule at AnneWilsonOfficial.com